BUREAUCRATS, CLIENTS, AND GEOGRAPHY

THE BAILLY NUCLEAR POWER PLANT BATTLE IN NORTHERN INDIANA

by

Nancy J. Obermeyer

National Center for Geographic Information and Analysis

University of Maine

UNIVERSITY OF CHICAGO

GEOGRAPHY RESEARCH PAPER NO. 216

1989

Library of Congress Cataloging-in-Publication Data

Obermeyer, Nancy J., 1955–
    Bureaucrats, clients, and geography : The Bailly nuclear power plant battle
in northern Indiana / by Nancy J. Obermeyer
        p.   cm. — (Geography research paper ; no. 216)
    Originally presented as the author's thesis.
    Includes bibliographical references (p.   ).
    ISBN 0-89065-121-3
    1. Land use—Government policy—United States—Decision making—Case
studies. 2. Land use—Government policy—United States—Citizen
participation—Case studies. 3. Pressure groups—United States—Case studies.
4. Bureaucracy—United States—Case studies. 5. Nuclear power plants—
United States—Location—Case studies. 6. U.S. Nuclear Regulatory
Commission. 7. Northern Indiana Public Service Company. I. Title. II.
Series: Geography research paper (Chicago, Ill.) ; no. 216.
HD205.024   1989   89-28824
333.73'13'0973—dc20   CIP

C

Geography Research Papers are available from:

The University of Chicago
Committee on Geographical Studies
5828 South University Avenue
Chicago, Illinois 60637-1583

In memory of my mother,
SHIRLEY AHR OBERMEYER

CONTENTS

CONTENTS

PREFACE

This monograph on the theme of organizational practices and their role in siting decisions was completed two years ago as my Ph.D. thesis at the University of Chicago. Of course, one can never be certain of the longevity of specific research hypotheses. It is easier to feel confident that one has chosen a worthwhile area for research.

My current work at the National Center for Geographic Information and Analysis (NCGIA) provides evidence of the usefulness of research on organizations and their role in geography. Since my arrival at the NCGIA, I have been struck by the growing importance of institutional and organizational issues to the development of geographical informations systems and their implementation in a mass market. As technical impediments to the expansion of GIS fall to research, institutional and organizational issues appear as additional hurdles.

It is my hope that this monograph will provide useful insight into the nature of the relationship between organizations and geography and stimulate additional research in this area.

ACKNOWLEDGMENTS

I would like to begin by expressing my sincere gratitude to my dissertation advisor, Professor Gordon L. Clark. From the time of his arrival at Chicago to the completion of this monograph, Professor Clark provided sound guidance and direction, offering both support and challenges as needed. I have learned a great deal from Professor Clark, and I consider it an honor to have been a student of his.

I also wish to thank other faculty members at the University of Chicago who played a role in this work, notably James Wescoat, who provided important direction on the environmental component of this paper; and Michael Conzen, who joined my committee in the latter stages of my work and provided additional guidance.

I would also like to express my appreciation to several individuals who were involved in the Bailly controversy and provided comments on an earlier draft of this monograph. Among them, Mark Reshkin and James Newman of Indiana University Northwest provided valuable insight into the conflict. Phil Phelan of the Northern Indiana Public Service Company and Jan Strasma of the U.S. Nuclear Regulatory Commission also provided valuable comments.

A special thanks to my dear friend, Lee Kednay, who introduced me to the Dunes.

In addition, I recognize the contributions of former teachers and professors who encouraged me over the years, including Professor Marjorie Randon Hershey, an inspirational undergraduate role model at Indiana University; Professor Howard A. Stafford, my M.A. thesis advisor at the University of Cincinnati; and Professors John Hudson and Breandán Ó hUallacháin, who gave me advice and encouragement while I was a teaching assistant at Northwestern University. To you and many others, thank you.

My thanks also goes to my husband, Samory Rashid, who has been my companion through completion of this project, and who has himself been similarly engaged during this period, and has thus provided knowing support through all the trials and tribulations.

Finally, I wish to express my appreciation to my parents, James J. and Shirley A. Obermeyer, who set a good example in their love of reading and learning, laying the groundwork for this effort.

Part 1

Chapter 1

INTRODUCTION

Little has been done in the past to apply the work done in the field of organizations to geography, yet there is great potential in doing so. By applying principles developed by organization theorists and experts in public administration to their public policy studies, geographers can better understand the power structures that form the foundations of public policy. Geographers are beginning to recognize that in order to understand public policy, they must first understand the policymakers, and to do that requires an understanding of bureaucratic organizations.

Beginning with Max Weber's theory of bureaucracy, this paper seeks to gain additional understanding of the actions of public organizations in general, and the Nuclear Regulatory Commission in particular. Weberian theory posits that a major source of a bureaucracy's power is its continuing good relationship with its clientele—people whose individual goals are the same as the bureaucracy's. Weber theorizes that the relationship between an organization and its client group is one of mutual dependency: each needs the other to survive and/or flourish.[1]

Background

In recent years, geographers have developed many excellent models to help them understand siting decisions and land-use patterns. The proliferation of and relatively easy access to computer hardware and software (including geographic information systems—GISs) have made it possible to

---

[1] H.H. Gerth, and C.W. Mills, *From Max Weber: Essays in Sociology* (New York: Oxford University Press, 1946), pp. 196-244. (Section 7, "Bureaucracy," is reprinted almost verbatim in Max Weber, *Economy and Society,* ed. Guenther Ross and Claus Wittich [Berkeley: University of California Press, 1978], pp. 956-1005. Gerth and Mills are credited as translators in this edition.)

develop highly complex models. These models can be used not only to explain how and why things are where they are, but can be implemented as prescriptions to siting and land-use problems. Models of this nature could be extremely useful in producing optimal solutions to questions of siting and land use.

Why, then, does so much conflict arise over siting and land-use issues in the public arena?

This book takes the position that other factors, not readily calculable, form an important part of decision-making on public siting and land use. The development of any type of quantitative model takes for granted that the model both can and will be implemented. Perhaps better outcomes would result if such models were routinely used; perhaps better siting and land-use decisions would result. Unfortunately (or not, depending on your perspective), this is not the case, particularly in the public arena.

In reality, siting decisions are usually left up to nongeographers who often do not have the thorough knowledge and understanding of geographical siting models to produce optimal siting decisions. Moreover, the people who make decisions are often members of organizations and as such, are subject to specific kinds of organizational pressures. Many siting decisions are either made or approved by public agencies operating under bureaucratic processes. This paper explores one such instance, the siting of a nuclear generating facility adjacent to the Indiana Dunes National Lakeshore, focusing on the relationship between the Nuclear Regulatory Commission and its client groups, a public utility and a group opposed to the facility. Evidence taken from NRC decisions on the site, along with research on the organization-client relationship, suggest that the bureaucracy's relationship with its client group plays a role in decision-making.

Methodology

This research uses a case-study approach to examine the problem. The case under study involves the decision of the Northern Indiana Public Service Company to site a nuclear generating facility (known as "Bailly") adjacent to the Indiana Dunes National Lakeshore. The Bailly case is of special interest because it involves a public organization pulled from two sides (the Atomic Energy Commission and its successor, the Nuclear Regulatory Commission—AEC/NRC). On one side is the Northern Indiana Public Service Company (NIPSCO); on the other, a group of private organizations and individuals concerned with environmental, health, and safety issues, the Joint Intervenors (JI). Both client groups were knowledgeable of the bureaucratic rules of the game and sophisticated in their use of those rules in their attempts to influence the outcome of the NRC's administrative decisions. Ironically, in the end, it was not the NRC, but economics that determined the siting choice, as the utility was forced to abandon its plans to build the facility, citing rising construction costs.

My methodology involved two strategies. The primary strategy was to examine all the AEC/NRC administrative decisions in the case, beginning with the its decision in 1972 to grant the utility a permit to construct the Bailly nuclear generating facility and ending with its decision in 1982 to require the utility to restore the construction site to its original condition. By and large, these decisions did not involve substantive environmental issues, but centered on administrative challenges filed by the JI as a strategy to postpone construction.

The second strategy was to discuss the case with the actors in order to verify basic information and analytical conclusions. These discussions, involving representatives of the NRC, NIPSCO, and the JI, supported the findings from the decisions. This research seeks especially to identify a plausible linkage between the AEC/NRC and its clients.

Max Weber's theory of bureaucracy provides a framework for seeking this linkage, and the organizational history of the AEC/NRC plays a critical role. Beginning its organizational life as a promoter of nuclear energy (the Atomic Energy Commission), the agency had more than a passing interest in the continued well-being of nuclear energy generally along with the well-being of the utility. In fact, as will be shown, throughout much of its life, the AEC/NRC was dogged by charges of conflict of interest on this very dimension. It is also germane to this research that during the debate over the Bailly site, the Atomic Energy Commission was reorganized to address those charges, with the Nuclear Regulatory Commission taking over the agency's regulatory functions and the Energy Research and Development Administration (ERDA) taking over the agency's promotional responsibilities.

A second factor of concern is the nature of the regulatory body itself. Regulatory agencies, in contrast to other agents of the state, possess an unusually broad grant of powers that spans the grant of authority extended by the U.S. Constitution to all three branches of government. Moreover, the highly technical nature of the NRC's jurisdiction has discouraged justices who rule on NRC actions from overturning NRC decisions on a technical basis. Indeed, judicial oversight of the NRC has been largely confined to administrative and procedural, rather than substantive, issues.

The Research Question

In arriving at my research question and devising an approach to carry out my analysis, I have reviewed literature in the fields of geography and public administration; I have read legal decisions in both administrative and federal courts; and I have learned about the actors involved. The research question stated below and my approach toward its exploration are the results of serious consideration of the general subject of the relationship between a bureaucracy and its client group. Specifically, this research discusses the regulatory bureaucracy.

Research question: How does the organization-client relationship affect locational decision-making?

The Bailly case is of special interest because it involves a public organization pulled from two sides. As the administrative body charged with the responsibility for executing nuclear siting decisions, the NRC must choose between opposing clientele groups in virtually every decision. The potential for struggle between the agency's clients is great. This struggle suggests a hypothesis and counterhypothesis to explain how the organization-client relationship affects locational decision-making.

Hypothesis A: A client group suggested by the the enabling framework (and mission) of the agency will dominate the locational decisions of that agency.

Counterhypothesis A: A client group that has historically enjoyed a close working relationship with the agency will dominate the locational decisions of that agency.

Null hypothesis A: The relationship between the organization and its clientele has no influence in the organization's decisions.

If Hypothesis A is accurate, then we would expect the Atomic Energy Commission (the NRC's predecessor until 1974) to favor the public utility, while the NRC's decisions should favor the group opposed to the Bailly facility. If Counterhypothesis A holds true, then we would expect the decisions of the NRC to favor the utility throughout the long conflict.

These hypotheses are concerned with the question of what constitutes a client group. On the one hand, there seems to be a "rightful" clientele. On the other hand, however, the client group may over time be determined by a "rule of capture." As I will show, the organization may find an advantage in allowing itself to be captured by a powerful client: capture by a powerful client can help assure the survival of the organization.

The other part of the equation is the client group itself. Of the two client groups involved, one (NIPSCO) had the benefit of a strong formal organizational structure. NIPSCO is a private, for-profit body to which the State of Indiana has granted the right to be the monopoly producer and seller of energy in the northwest corner of the state. The utility has a steady revenue derived from its sale of energy. It also has a full-time paid staff.

These factors, along with the expertise of its staff, combine to make NIPSCO the expert on energy needs for the region.

Opposing the utility was an ad hoc group, the Joint Intervenors, a group of residents of Dune Acres, Indiana, who objected to having a nuclear power facility literally in their backyards. This group named themselves the Concerned Citizens Against Bailly Nuclear Power Station. Over the years of the Bailly controversy, the ranks of the JI swelled to include these additional groups:

Izaak Walton League (Porter County, Indiana, chapter)
The Lake Michigan Federation
The Save the Dunes Council
The Bailly Alliance
The Critical Mass Energy Project
Businessmen for the Public Interest, Inc. (later renamed Business and
    Professional People for the Public Interest)
The State of Illinois
The City of Gary
United Steelworkers (Locals 1010 and 6787)

Although these participants were united on the single issue of the Bailly plant, they were not necessarily united on any other issue or in their stated organizational missions. Even though these groups did not exist as a single bloc with a united cause, both administrative and federal courts nevertheless granted them standing to sue NIPSCO. The JI gained their legitimacy and legal standing on the basis of their claim that they represented a legitimate public interest.

The differing sources of legitimacy of NIPSCO and the Joint Intervenors suggest a second hypothesis and counterhypothesis to explain how the organization-client relationship affects locational decision-making.

Hypothesis B: A client whose existence and organizational structure are determined by formal and legal means will tend to dominate organizational location decisions by virtue of its strong organizational structure.

Counterhypothesis B: A client group that owes its existence to its commitment to speak on behalf of a legitimate public interest will tend to dominate the locational decisions of public organizations.

Null hypothesis B: The source of a client's legitimacy plays no role in its ability to influence the locational decisions of public agencies.

If Hypothesis B is accurate, then we would expect the AEC/NRC's decisions to favor NIPSCO. If the counterhypothesis holds true, then we would expect the NRC's decisions to reflect public opinion on nuclear power. That is, during the early seventies, in light of the Arab oil embargo of 1973 and the ensuing energy crisis, the NRC's decisions should favor

NIPSCO. At the end of the decade, which was marked by the nuclear accident at Three Mile Island, the agency's decisions should tend to favor the JI.

Indeed, what this research indicates is that an organization responds to various pressures, not the least of which is the pressure exerted by client groups. In general, however, the organization tends to favor its captor, usually a dynamic and well-directed entity. But in certain instances, the organization can respond to the needs and wants of a more generalized public interest. Periodically, conflict-of-interest concerns compel the organization to renew its public legitimacy as a means of assuring its organizational survival. This it does by responding to the public interest as expressed, for example, by collective action.

The regulatory agency presents an especially interesting case because of its relative autonomy. Unlike most public agencies, the regulator is not constrained by separation-of-power limitations. Regulators can promulgate rules and execute them; regulators are also the first-line adjudicators of their own rules. In the case of the NRC, the agency itself contains an appeals process. It is only after exhausting internal agency appeals that litigants may take their cases to the federal judicial system. Even when litigants appeal cases involving the NRC in the courts, judges routinely limit their reviews of decisions to purely procedural concerns, deferring to the expertise of NRC professionals on technical questions and issues.

This is not to suggest that NRC decisions are arbitrary and capricious. Indeed, the NRC has its own formulas and models which it uses as a basis for siting decisions. Two points must be made concerning such formulas and models. First, it is possible to disagree with the factors and their weightings in siting formulas. Second, even if there were general agreement on the models and formulas used, variations in implementation of those models produce varying results.

Such was the case at Bailly. A study performed by Richard Hansis, professor of geography at Valparaiso University, indicated that the method used to calculate safety zones for the Bailly facility was highly questionable. His findings indicated that in order to obtain a zone of population densities low enough to win a construction permit, the NRC had permitted the utility to include a sizable portion of (unpopulated) Lake Michigan in its calculations. Had Lake Michigan been excluded from the formula, a different conclusion would have resulted, namely, the site chosen would have been unacceptable according to the NRC's own standards.

The Chapters

Decisions on public siting and land use are of great importance to geographers. This book attempts to shed additional light on how these decisions come to be and why geographically optimal decisions are not always the rule. The chapters that follow will explore the interaction between regulators and their clients and examine the impact of that interaction on siting and land-use decisions, using the Bailly case as an example.

The following three chapters constitute Part 1, the purpose of which is to lay the foundation for the case study. Chapter 2, "Geography and the Administrative State," identifies the body of geographic literature into which this research is intended to fit. The organization does not operate in a vacuum, but rather plays by specific rules and norms established within a specific governmental arrangement. Those rules and norms limit and direct the public organization in its actions. This chapter discusses how geographers have viewed those rules and norms. By and large, geographers have failed to establish a relationship between state form and function. The exception is the work of Clark and Dear, whose *State Apparatus* does just that. This research goes one step further, to discuss a specific organizational form within the state that is an additional source of influence on outcomes.

Following up on this more generalized discussion, chapter 3, "The Administrative Bureaucracy," describes a particular organizational form and discusses how that form influences outcomes. Beginning with a review of Weber's theory of bureaucracy, this chapter reviews the literature on the organization-client relationship, and attempts to build a case for using this theory to enlighten the geographical literature on the administrative state. Finally, this chapter attempts to develop a theory of the relationship between the regulatory agency and its clients. The fourth chapter, "Legal Environment of the Regulatory Agency," sets out to place the regulator within its appropriate legal constraints. As will be made clear, the regulatory agency has a surprising level of autonomy. It is because of this autonomy that the regulator's relationship with its clients is especially interesting.

Part 2 details the case study. Chapter 5, "Background: Overview and Actors," attempts to provide a geographical and historical perspective for the case study. As will be shown, the Indiana Dunes are a region of both economic and environmental significance to the state. Moreover, this region is not a stranger to controversy, the conflict over Bailly being a reprise of earlier debates. Chapter 5 provides background on the organization and clients involved in the Bailly case study. Three actors are discussed: the rise of the AEC and its later reorganization into the NRC and the ERDA form the major part of this chapter, which also includes brief discussions of the clients involved, NIPSCO and the JI. The next chapter, "The Bailly Decisions," chronicles the Bailly case from the time of NIPSCO's application for a construction permit to its decision to abandon the facility. This case extended from 1972 until 1982 and was highly litigious. This chapter details the challenges that the JI brought against the Bailly facility, along with the relevant AEC/NRC decisions.

"Analysis" and "Conclusions" form the elements of Part 3. In "Analysis," I both examine the NRC decisions as they reflect the relationship between an organization and its clients, and discuss the hypotheses presented above. In "Conclusions," I attempt to bring further clarity to the nature of the relationship between organizations and their clients, and finally, I suggest how the knowledge gained from this research may be used to inform geographical theory on siting and land-use questions.

Chapter 2

GEOGRAPHY AND THE ADMINISTRATIVE STATE

Because the rules and regulations that govern the Bailly case are of the state's making, theories of the state warrant serious review. While current theories of the state discuss its form and function, by and large they fail to provide an adequate link between the two. I suggest that the link is a state apparatus, specifically bureaucratic administration. This chapter attempts to make a case for that bureaucratic link, building upon recent geographical literature on the theory of the state as a framework.

A theory of the state should tell us something about the form and function of the state. The state includes all three branches of government as defined by traditional U.S. civics courses: executive and administrative, representative (legislative), and judicial. Comprehensive theories of the state may seek to describe, explain, or predict the relationships between and among the three branches of government. Particularistic theories may instead emphasize the operations of a single branch or even of a smaller unit within one of the branches.

Why is it important to develop a theory of the state within the discipline of geography? Johnston emphasizes the variance over space of state spending and regulatory functions as the primary reason for the importance of a theory of the state to geography.[1] Other state functions (including revenue collection) also vary over space. Whereas Johnston's concern is focused predominantly on the function of the state (for example, on the state's role as regulator in environmental issues), form is also important. Like function, state form may also vary over space, which may in turn have an influence on how state functions are implemented over space.

---

[1] R.J. Johnston, *Geography and the State* (New York: St. Martin's Press, 1982).

The approach adopted in this chapter presumes the existence of a state whose form and functions influence geographical patterns. There are those who would prefer to take an "original position" perspective, arguing that the existence of a state in general, and of a specific type of state in particular, is not to be taken for granted. My response is this: the United States, within whose border this study takes place, is a nation whose government was established some two hundred years ago. It is a relatively stable entity with the capacity to influence society. However, I do not deny the interaction of the society and the government. The relationship between the state and society is both dynamic and mutually dependent, creating diverse outcomes over both space and time.

The contemporary approach in the geographic literature to the study of the state owes as much to what Willbern calls the "new public administration"[2] as it does to the type of research performed by early political geographers. The new public administration (New PA) marks its beginnings in the late 1960s and early 1970s and had as one of its outward manifestations the founding of several major centers for the study of public administration in the United States in the early seventies. Prominent among these centers are the Indiana University School of Public and Environmental Affairs (1971); Harvard's John F. Kennedy School of Government (1973); the University of Texas LBJ School of Public Affairs; and the University of Minnesota Humphrey Institute of Public Affairs.

Campbell marks three separate stages in the development of public administration since World War II, culminating in the New PA.[3] The first stage can be further broken down into two phases. During the first phase, young public administrators were sent to the Office of Price Administration and the Office of Strategic Services armed with the four basic principles of public administration: (1) the separation of policy and administration, (2) the significance of the formal organization, (3) the value of professionalism, and (4) the need for value neutrality.

Returning from their war experience older and wiser, these seasoned public administrators learned that policy and administration are not separable. The manner in which policy is administered can influence the nature of the policy that is implemented. They learned that organizational charts do not always accurately identify the flow of influence within the organization. Finally, they learned that politics permeate all levels of the organization, making value neutrality little more than illusion.

---

[2] Y. Willbern, "Types and Levels of Public Morality," *Public Administration Review*, v. 44, n. 2 (March-April 1984): 102-8.

[3] A.K. Campbell, "Old and New Public Administration in the 1970s," *Public Administration Review*, v. 32, n. 4 (July-August 1972): 343-47.

This learning precipitated a period of empirical examination of administrative practice. In time, this empiricism manifested itself in a quantitative revolution similar to that which occurred in geography and the other social sciences. This constituted the second stage, which was dominated by a group of scholars who could be characterized as refiners of and builders on earlier public administration principles that emphasized scientific management and efficiency. The emphasis was on finding the "one best way" to perform administrative tasks.

A reorientation in the field began in the early 1960s, then came into full flower in the late 1960s and early 1970s. Under the vision of the New PA, the basic principles of professionalism, credentialism, hierarchy, and authority were all challenged. These principles were replaced by doctrines of citizen participation, client control, decentralization, neighborhood government, and value consciousness. The New PA has two basic orientations: internal and external. The internal orientation emphasizes the arrangement of the organization, particularly attacking the concept of the significance of the formal organization, and replacing it with the notion that interpersonal relationships within the organization are also important. The external orientation emphasizes the role of the organization as a public servant of its client group and the accountability of the organization to its clients.

Like any newly forming subdiscipline, that of geography and the state suffers from growing pains coming from a lack of clear direction. Geographers can gain valuable insight from the recent developments in the field of public administration, whose practitioners have many years of experience in the analysis of state form and function. Conversely, by applying their own specifically geographical expertise and approach to PA research, geographers can make significant contributions to research on the state.

I have four major criticisms of the literature on geography and the state. First and foremost there seems to be no cohesive theory of geography and the state, but rather analysis currently exists in an eclectic form. Second, virtually all of the literature on geography and the state has taken a functionalist approach while ignoring the underlying structures responsible for carrying out those functions. Third, while focusing on the public sector, few authors have considered seriously the important differences between the public and private sectors, and those who have done so routinely underestimate the ramifications of those differences. Finally, the literature of geography and the state has underrated the effects of the organization and its behavior on policy.

It is my intention in this chapter not only to critique the literature of geography and the state and to elaborate the above criticisms, but also to

suggest that by adopting a viewpoint acknowledging the existence c
bureaucratic organizations, their roles, structure, and behavior, geographers
can advance their study of the state.

Setting the Stage

As previously noted, geography and the state, in one form or
another, have a long history together. It is important, however, to recognize
a shift in approach from early political geographers to contemporary
research on the state by geographers, a shift that more or less replicates the
shift from traditional public administration to the New PA. For this reason,
my literature review emphasizes research on geography and the state that
coincides with the development of the New PA.

In 1976, Brian J.L. Berry noted that "Geographers have made few, if
any, significant contributions to the formulation or evaluation of urban
policy, and the essays in this book are offered as one small step toward re-
dressing the situation."[4] With that, Berry introduced *Urban Policymaking
and Metropolitan Dynamics: A Comparative Geographical Analysis*, a collection of a baker's dozen essays on urban policy commissioned by the
Association of American Geographers. Berry's introductory essay, "On
Geography and Urban Policy," takes the view that geographers can play an
important role in urban policy development and evaluation through serious research efforts. Berry continues, "Perhaps the most important influence that good research can have on policy development is through its
effects on the way policymakers look at the world."[5]

Although Berry's essay remains an important challenge to urban and
administrative geographers, it was not the first. In his 1970 article, Robert B.
McNee acknowledged the powerful role played by "big government" along
with "big business" and "big labor" in locational decision-making in the
United States. McNee called upon geographers to review the literature on
organizations and to combine it with their geographical expertise to develop
a geographical approach to the study of public policy in order to "compre-
hend the bureaucratic age in which we live."[6] McNee expressed the need for
geographers to enhance their capabilities as planners in business and
government. He emphasized the need for geographers to accept some
degree of social responsibility for the geographic functioning of the system
in which we operate. Finally, he called for geographers to become social

---

[4]   B.J.L. Berry, "On Geography and Urban Policy," in *Urban Policymaking and Metropolitan Dynamics: A Comparative Geographical Analysis*, ed. John S. Adams (Cambridge,
Mass.: Ballinger, 1976), p. 3.

[5]   Ibid., p. 4.

[6]   R.N. McNee, "Regional Planning, Bureaucracy, and Geography," *Economic Geography*, v.
46, n. 2 (April 1970): 192.

critics when necessary, using "geographical expertise to examine critically the locational decisions being made by the multitudinous planning bodies."[7]

Two years later, Gilbert F. White noted that up to that time, the AAG had given very little attention to the problems of public policy during what seemed to him to be a period of crisis in the United States. He applauded the efforts of a small group of geographers who were concentrating their research efforts on the problems of urban blight.

Dear made an important contribution when he recognized that geographers needed to develop a new perspective and new criteria if they were to study and evaluate issues in the public sector. Dear noted the distinctive context of the location of public (as opposed to private) facilities, drawing attention to the public sector emphasis on equity (in contrast to economic efficiency), the lack of competition in the public sector, and the need for public accountability and input in the decisions of public agencies. In addition, he recognized the importance of studying organizations as a way to enhance our understanding of public actions. Finally, Dear acknowledged the political nature of public locational decision-making.[8] One would expect that such a strong case for a public/private distinction would lead to a reorientation of perspective in the geographical literature. Unfortunately, this has not been the case, as Dear's advice has been largely ignored.

For the most part, in fact, these very early calls for the study of public policy went unheeded. Berry's challenge, too, went unanswered in the first year or two after it was issued. It was not until the late 1970s that these exhortations for research in public policy by geographers began to bear fruit consistently and in any number.

Among the most important geographic literature on the state is a 1978 article by Dear and Clark, in which the authors identify five major interpretations of the role of the state in geographic processes. These five roles are: (1) supplier of public goods and services, (2) facilitator and regulator of the economy, (3) social engineer, (4) arbiter, and (5) agent of some ruling elite.[9] The fifth is essentially a Marxist theory of the state.

Contending that the state will act in the interests of all members of a capitalist class society, Dear and Clark are not surprised by reformist policies that do not directly serve the interest of the capitalist state, and they interpret such policies as long-term strategies of crisis avoidance, necessitated by the inevitable incidence of class antagonisms. The authors prefer, however,

---

[7] Ibid., p. 98.

[8] M.J. Dear, "A Paradigm for Public Facility Location Theory," *Antipode*, v. 6, n. 1 (April 1974).

[9] M.J. Dear and G.L. Clark, "The State and Geographic Process: A Critical Review," *Environment and Planning-A*, v. 10, n. 2 (February 1978).

to view the state both as an independent entity, with its own function and goals, and as an integral component of the set of power relations that comprise capitalist society.[10]

Theories of the State

In the early seventies, geographers began the arduous process of developing general theories of the state, tending to focus on the development of its specific forms (e.g., Dikshit's study of federalism) and functions (such as the previously mentioned work by Dear and Clark). As will become apparent, there is virtually no effort in the literature to link form with function, a situation that calls for rectification. Still, the literature does provide some basic building blocks in its initial stages which, as the process of theory-building continues, can be cemented together to form a solid foundation upon which later theory can stand.

State Form and Outcomes

An important work that predates much of the geographical literature on the state, Ramesh D. Dikshit's "Geography and Federalism" helps to lay a firm foundation for the study of the state. By understanding the underlying themes of federalism, we can in turn understand some of the basic conflicts underlying the structure of the state in the United States.

Dikshit contends that a federation is created when two or more separate or autonomous political units agree to join together into a single state with a sovereign central government, but retain for themselves some degree of regional autonomy. In a federation, the legislative and executive powers are divided between the federal (central) and the unit (regional) governments, with each government acting directly on the people.[11]

The federal system is a dynamic system, says Dikshit, a compromise between centrifugal and centripetal forces acting concurrently. As long as the states can neither separate without losing the advantages of union (such as defense or economic benefits) nor fully unite without forgoing highly valued individual identities, the political units create a sort of halfway house between absolute unity and complete separation, with the result being a federation.

Dikshit views the modern federation as a functional creature, its primary purposes being the performance of tasks and the provision of services. In order to achieve its purposes, the federation requires a great deal of con-

---

[10] Ibid.

[11] R.D. Dikshit, "Geography and Federalism," *Annals of the Association of American Geographers*, v. 61, n. 1 (January-February 1971).

tinuing cooperation, particularly in light of the growing involvement of the federal government in state and local matters that occurred in the United States in the sixties and seventies.

In discussing the form of the federal system, Dikshit quotes Grodzins: "The American form of government is often, but erroneously, symbolized by a three-layer cake. A far more correct image is the rainbow or marble cake, characterized by an inseparable intermingling of differently coloured ingredients, the colours apparently in vertical and diagonal strands and unexpected swirls. As colours are mixed in a marble cake, so functions are mixed in the American federal system."[12]

Dikshit describes two types of federalism. In a system of dual federalism, the central and unit governments are equal rivals. In cooperative federalism, they are equal partners. The distinction between the two types of federalism may be definitionally clear, but in practice, the federal system in the United States is a mix of the two, containing elements of both intergovernmental rivalry and cooperation.

Dikshit considers federalism to be the most geographically expressive form of government. He posits two reasons. First, the emergence of a federation can come only where regional differences exist and are recognized. If there were no differences, a more unified state would result. Second, the regions in a federation tend to remain highly articulated and recognizable, even after federation has occurred. The basic geographical premise of federalism is the existence and recognition of the diversity of regional groups.

Dikshit's study of federalism is important because it brings out the theme of states' rights versus federal authority and provides some explanation for the inherent conflict between them. When we speak of the state, we cannot ignore the existence of a hierarchy (however muddled) of institutions, nor can we deny the difficulties resulting from that hierarchy. This theme is reflected in later literature (especially the work of Clark, Dear, and others) that explores issues of local autonomy.

State form and function individually continue to be important in later literature of geographical theories of the state. Dear contends that two issues will dominate the research agenda in the field: the form of the state and the functions of state apparatus. Dear defines form as the way in which a specific state structure is constituted and evolves in a given social formation. He defines function as both the way in which and the reason why state power is exercised through particular institutions.[13]

---

[12] Ibid., p. 103.

[13] M.J. Dear, "The State: A Research Agenda," *Environment and Planning-A*, v. 13, n. 10 (October 1981).

Dear identifies separable tiers comprising state apparatus. The primary tier, representing the minimum requirements necessary for the exercise of state power, includes a repressive enforcement branch and an administrative branch that takes in the bureaucratic machinery of the state. The secondary tier is composed of the enabling apparatuses of the state, including its legal, political, and cultural-welfare mechanisms.

Dear calls for research relating to state form and function in five separate segments of the government: government bureaucracy; repression and welfare as state ideologies; politics and the language of the state; the local state; and law and the state. Dear was criticized, however, on two counts, neither directly relating to his call for research. The first criticism was a charge that he had applied the concept of capitalism in an uncritical way. He was also criticized for his assumption that a liberal state will always lead to a situation wherein the predominant mode of producing goods and services is commercial.[14] In spite of these criticisms, Dear's call for research on the state continues to be one of the most compelling, and his concept of state form one of the most intriguing.

Growing out of Dear's article are several other articles on local autonomy. Johnston discusses the role of the judicial branch in the autonomy issue. Focusing on the U.S. experience, he describes a situation wherein the actions of local managers may be subject to scrutiny by the Supreme Court, which he describes as a panel of "supermanagers." As a set of managers, he continues, the Supreme Court has an important influence on attitudes toward certain issues within American society. Its power to enforce those attitudes and thereby to influence the nation's geography, however, is variable.[15] This view of the Supreme Court justices as supermanagers is probably mistaken, particularly given the distance of the justices from the implementation of their decisions. Rather than manage, the justices carry on their traditional role as arbiters, a role that is certainly an influential one.

A more theoretical discussion of autonomy was presented by Dear and Clark in 1981. According to the authors, a materialist theory of the capitalist state construes the local state to be an apparatus of crisis management and of ideological hegemony over spatially extensive and heterogeneous jurisdictions. Their evidence from the state of Massachusetts confirms the notion that local state autonomy is subordinate to central state authority.[16]

---

[14] D.G. Green, "The Spatial Sciences and the State," *Environment and Planning-A*, v. 14, n. 11 (November 1982).

[15] R.J. Johnston, "The Management and Autonomy of the Local State: The Role of the Judiciary in the U.S.," *Environment and Planning-A*, v. 13, n. 10 (October 1981).

[16] M.J. Dear and G.L. Clark, "Dimensions of Local State Autonomy," *Environment and Planning-A*, v. 13, n. 10 (October 1981).

The state uses two functional components to achieve ideological hegemony, the authors contend. These components are electoral politics and the state bureaucracy. Dear and Clark further describe state bureaucracy as perhaps the most significant cooptive mechanism in contemporary capitalism. They suggest that it is possible to view the bureaucracy as being composed of agents who "obfuscate the system of authority and control in capitalist social relations both vertically (across the various state levels) and horizontally (between the various local state jurisdictions and the different, though ideologically related, branches of the political and executive authorities)."[17] One must be cautious, however, to avoid stereotyping bureaucracy as an inherently evil perpetrator of sloth, inefficiency, waste, and generalized malfeasance. At the same time, it is important to recognize the significance of this article, for it continues to stand virtually alone among the geographical literature in its discussion of bureaucracy.

Johnston again tries his hand at developing a theory of the state, and points out that the geographer has ample reason to be interested in state activity because many state spending and regulatory functions vary over space. Discussing functions of the state, he lists six: (1) protector, (2) arbitrator, (3) cohesive force (characterized by nationalism or patriotism), (4) facilitator (relating to the provision of infrastructure), (5) investor (in education, in financing research, and in providing subsidies to firms), and (6) bureaucracy.[18]

Rather than describe bureaucracy as a separate function of the state, perhaps a more accurate assessment is that bureaucracy is the agent of the state that implements the first five functions Johnston identifies. This distinction (elaborated below) is an important step toward developing a comprehensive theory of the state.

The state bureaucracy and its employees, Johnston says, are probably the most visible indication of the existence of a state. Following the work of Weber, Johnston contends that once created, the bureaucracy takes on a rationale (and a life) of its own. He views the bureaucracy as a vested interest group that has considerable power within society growing from the functions it performs. He further believes that the bureaucracy desires to maintain—and if possible to increase—its power in order to preserve the wellbeing of the operators of the state (the bureaucrats) both individually and collectively. This idea forms the major theme of this book and is discussed explicitly in chapter 3.

---

[17] Ibid., p. 1282.

[18] R.J. Johnston, *Geography and the State* (New York: St. Martin's Press, 1982).

Johnston had introduced this idea earlier in his book *Political, Electoral and Spatial Systems: An Essay in Political Geography*.[19] He goes on to discuss two theoretical approaches to the study of state decision-making. The first approach, pluralism, prevails in a democracy where all voices are heard. The second approach, managerialism, posits that decisions are made by managers, rather than by elected officials. Managers make decisions based not only on demands placed on them by outside sources, but also on their own self-interest and ideologies.

Again following Weber, Johnston discusses the professionalism of local managers. In theory, he says, they are public servants. In practice, however, they come closer to being rulers because of their substantive knowledge and expertise and their ability to use this knowledge to their best advantage. In contrast to the elected officials, who are nominally masters of the bureaucracy, and who are likely to be technically ignorant (Weber would call them dilettantes), the bureaucrat is hired because of his or her expertise and thus finds himself or herself in a position of relative power.

Johnston's work stands out because of his Weberian approach to the study of bureaucracies, an approach that had been previously overlooked in the geographical literature. Dear praised Johnston for his successful demonstration of the need to situate the topics of political geography within a wider context of the state. He goes on, however, to criticize Johnston on the grounds that his (Johnston's) theory of the state never resolves the contradictions between corporatism, pluralism, managerialism, and instrumentalism.[20] Clark criticizes Johnston's eclecticism, noting that the author describes no theory of the state.[21] Still, Johnston's book is important for its advancement of the notion that the study of the state and its institutions is crucial to the advancement of geographical thought, as well as for its inclusion of Weber's theory of bureaucracy.

Two other anthologies promise more than they deliver with regard to theories of the state. In *Political Studies from Spatial Perspectives*, the editors, Burnett and Taylor, begin with a general theory of the state that posits that governments exist in order to make collective social choices pertaining to the provision of economic goods and services that in consumption possess the properties of what economists refer to as public

---

[19] R.J. Johnston, *Political, Electoral and Spatial Systems: An Essay in Political Geography* (Oxford: Oxford University Press, 1979).

[20] M.J. Dear, Review of *Geography and the State*, by R.J. Johnston, *Environment and Planning-A*, v. 15, n. 10 (October 1983).

[21] G.L. Clark, Review of *Geography and the State*, by R.J. Johnston, *Environment and Planning D: Society and Space*, v. 1, n. 4 (1983).

goods.[22] This volume is as eclectic as its title implies, largely concentrating on voting patterns and boundary issues, rather than on theories of the state. Another anthology, *Institutions and Geographical Patterns*, also begins with good intentions but ends in the disappointment of eclecticism. In the introductory section, Flowerdew and his coauthor, Thomas Manion, state their belief that an institutional approach to geography should seek to develop theory concerning the impact of institutional controls on the activities of individuals or companies and the resulting spatial patterns.[23] The editor, however, makes no effort to develop any theory or to unify the diverse individual articles in the book in any way.

There are several important themes running through the literature on theories of the state: form, function, autonomy, and bureaucracy. As previously noted, these themes remain largely unconnected in the literature, although they are quite interconnected in reality. Dikshit's work on the federal form clearly brings out the concept of central versus regional state control, which is closely related to the issue of autonomy, discussed by several authors. Autonomy has two basic components: responsibility and authority. Responsibility refers to the obligation of a unit of government to provide services. Authority refers to the degree of power or control the unit may exercise over other units.

Autonomy, then is linked with function in both the delivery of services and the exercise of power. This important link is an agent of the state, its bureaucracy; and for the most part, it has been neglected by the geographical literature.

State Functions

By far the overwhelming emphasis in geographic literature of the state has been on the functions of the state. The state plays an important role in our daily routines, providing a good many services and regulating various aspects of our lives. Perhaps this is one reason for the predominance of the functionalist approach: state function is a clear manifestation of state form over geographic space, and is thus an obvious point of interest for geographers.

Whatever the reason or reasons, geographers have done considerable research on the many and various functions of the state. This research, as will become evident, is not particularly unified, either with other functionalist literature in the field or with the rarer literature on general theories of

---

[22] A.D. Burnett and P.J. Taylor, eds., *Political Studies from Spatial Perspectives* (New York: John Wiley and Sons, 1981).

[23] R. Flowerdew, ed., *Institutions and Geographical Patterns* (New York: St. Martin's Press, 1982).

the state. Still, as we begin to view the functionalist literature as part of a larger body of literature on geography and the administrative state, its role within the larger view will become evident.

The State as Arbiter

Recent efforts by geographers have contributed to new ways of thinking about the state. According to the schema developed by Dear and Clark described earlier, the state's role as arbiter stems from its position within the context of conflicts in society, between elements of the state system as well as between social groups. The literature on the state's role as arbiter is closely related to the issue of autonomy. In certain cases, the question is one of strict constitutionality, wherein the federal government exercises ultimate authority. In other cases, the question is one of interregional diversity, wherein neither region directly involved may exercise autonomy over the other, necessitating intervention by a more powerful unit of government.

In his article "Law, the State, and the Spatial Integration of the United States,"[24] Clark argues that spatial integration can be viewed as an outgrowth of the debate among competing classes during the American Revolutionary period. At that time, the classes agreed that the basic unit of society was the individual, an agreement which has had a major impact on the American landscape, most strongly manifested in the American attitude toward private ownership of land.

That agreement has played a significant role in the subsequent development of spatial diversity in the United States. Clark develops a two-part thesis. First, he says, the spatial diversity of the United States has been systematically negated by the judiciary since about 1880. Later, as a consequence, space as a social and political concept is now virtually irrelevant in judicial action, as local autonomy has consistently lost out to the "national interest." Clark's discussion of the judicial role of the state is a major contribution to the study of geography and the state.[25]

Later, Fincher looked at the state's policies toward potentially contentious issues surrounding the built environment, and identified three themes: (1) the encouragement of citizens' interest groups, (2) the spatially differentiated targeting of public investment, and (3) the awarding of advantage to large-scale capital. These policies, she says, are partly influenced by individual policymakers. But they are also constrained by economic and political realities and their spatial manifestations in cities. In focusing on the constraints imposed by economic and political realities, Fincher rejects a

---

[24] G.L. Clark, "Law, the State and the Spatial Integration of the United States," *Environment and Planning-A,* v. 13, n. 10 (October 1981).
[25] Ibid.

conspiracy theory, wherein the agents of the local state and of large-scale development corporations are portrayed as villains, while local residents and smaller businesses are portrayed as victims.[26]

Eyles, Smith, and Woods, discussing the state's role as arbiter, contend that this role is not based solely on the political authority that the state derives from the social structure. Rather, social power and political authority are separate. The authors argue that the state is an administrative apparatus that makes technical decisions from its position outside its social order.[27] Like Johnston, these authors adopt a Weberian position.

The role of the state as arbiter is of particular importance in the U.S. federal system, as previously described by Dikshit. The existence of diverse regions and the hierarchical arrangement of governmental levels almost assure conflict requiring arbitration if the federation is to continue. It is surprising in this light that so little work has emphasized the state's role as arbiter.

The State as Supplier

The state's role as supplier has been an important theme in the literature on geography and the state. If one thinks of the state as a supplier of goods, it is easy to see that this role has clear geographical implications. Where does the state get the goods that it supplies, or the money it needs to purchase them? Where does it send the supplies? And why?

As the state's role as supplier has shown a simple link to geography, so have geographers taken a simplistic approach to this role. On the whole, the literature on the state as supplier is tightly focused, often exploring a single federal program or part of a program. As we will see, it is the rare article that attempts to integrate itself within a larger view of geography and the state.

One of the earliest, and most influential, articles on the state as supplier was written by Charles M. Tiebout in 1956. The Tiebout hypothesis, as it has come to be known, basically states that local governments have as their primary goal providing the "right goods" to their citizens. If the state fails in that goal, citizens will respond by taking the "exit option," that is, they will move away to a place where they can get the right goods.[28] The

---

26 R. Fincher, "Local Implementation Strategies in the Urban Built Environment," *Environment and Planning-A*, v. 13, n. 10 (October 1981).

27 J. Eyles, D.M. Smith, and K.J. Woods, "Spatial Resource Allocation and State Practice: The Case of Health Service Planning in London," *Regional Studies*, v. 16, n. 4 (1982).

28 C.M. Tiebout, "A Pure Theory of Local Expenditures," *Journal of Political Economy*, v. 64, n. 5 (1956).

research of Lindal[29], Samuelson,[30] and others describes the difficulty of assessing the value of pure public goods. While Tiebout's approach attempts to overcome these difficulties by using the exit option as a surrogate for the revealed public preferences for public goods, there remain several problems with the Tiebout hypothesis.

The Tiebout hypothesis went unchallenged for nearly twenty-five years, but three geographers have raised serious criticisms since 1980. The first, Bennett, criticized Tiebout's assumption that the exit option is always available. Raising issues such as zoning, building codes, and social or racial discrimination, Bennett noted that the economically efficient solutions predicted by Tiebout were unobtainable in practice.[31] Clark criticized Tiebout's assumption that local levels of government are strongest, noting that empirical evidence does not bear out this assumption. Clark also faulted Tiebout for excluding the role of democracy in the provision of public service.[32] Finally, Whiteman voiced several criticisms. Agreeing with Bennett, he acknowledged that moving is not always an option. Following Clark's comment on democracy, he noted that voting is another means by which citizens can voice their displeasure with local goods and services. In addition, Whiteman criticized Tiebout for his failure to acknowledge that there are other motives for moving besides the search for public goods. Finally, Whiteman faulted Tiebout for his omission of the role of the federal government in local government finance.[33] I would also add that while Tiebout attempts to overcome the inherent difficulties of trying to place a value on public goods, his "exit option" is, at best, a crude and imprecise method to achieve this objective. These challenges to the Tiebout hypothesis reaffirm the importance of recognizing the differences between the public and private sectors and the ramifications of those differences suggested by Dear and described earlier.[34]

Several authors have explored federal grant programs. Once again, the theme of autonomy as an expression of conflict between central and regional governments becomes important. In the case of federal grant programs, central governments offer assistance to regional units so that certain specified national goals may be furthered. In return for assistance, regional

---

[29] E. Lindal, "Just Taxation—A Positive Solution," in *Classics in the Economics of Public Finance,* ed. R. Musgrave and J. Peacock (London: Macmillan, 1958).

[30] P.A. Samuelson, "The Pure Theory of Public Expenditures," *Review of Economics and Statistics,* v. 36 (1954): 387-89.

[31] R.J. Bennett, *The Geography of Public Finance* (London: Methuen, 1980).

[32] G.L. Clark, "Law, the State, and the Spatial Integration of the United States," *Environment and Planning-A,* v. 13, n. 10 (October 1981).

[33] J. Whiteman, "Deconstructing the Tiebout Hypothesis," *Environment and Planning D: Society and Space,* v. 1, n. 3 (1983).

[34] Dear, "A Paradigm for Public Facility Location Theory."

units are nearly always expected—in fact required—to give up certain speci-fied rights. For example, states that accept federal aid for highway construc-tion must abide by the rules of the National Environmental Policy Act of 1969 and submit an Environmental Impact Statement (EIS). In general, states are precluded by the findings included in the EIS from building their roads along environmentally sensitive routes. Although the reader should be able to make the connection between the autonomy issue and the litera-ture on federal aid, the authors who write such articles are rarely so explicit.

An important early work on federal assistance is a 1969 article by Stanley D. Brunn and Wayne L. Hoffman, "The Geography of Federal Grants-in-Aid to States." The authors begin with the premise that in theory, the major reason why the federal government supports grant-in-aid pro-grams is to place all states a somewhat equal level with regard to certain specified rational objectives. Brunn and Hoffman then proceed to discuss the general aims and types of assistance to states, to illustrate the areal distri-bution of federal aid to states by selecting specific programs for consider-ation, and to examine the selected program outcomes with the help of maps and simple multiple-regression models.[35]

The authors draw several conclusions from their study. First, they conclude that over all programs they studied, the places that won the greatest per capita grant awards were states with low population densities, low median incomes, small urban populations, and relatively limited agri-cultural and manufacturing bases. Antipoverty funds taken alone, how-ever, tended to go to states with low median incomes, low education levels, high percentages of population in the poverty class, and relatively un-healthy manufacturing and agricultural bases when compared to the rest of the nation. The authors' findings suggest that federal grant programs are well targeted to achieve their primary purpose.

Wohlenberg has written two separate articles (1976 and 1979) on the system of public welfare grants in the United States. The earlier work de-scribes a study of the rate of success of state-administered programs on the basis of eight different factors that fall into two general categories: ambient political geography and local fiscal ability. Using regression analytic tech-niques, Wohlenberg determines that the effectiveness of public assistance programs in every state was well below the ideal one-hundred percent level. He finds also that the lack of total effectiveness can be traced to insufficient federal funds flowing into the state welfare program, and suggests that funding criteria be altered in such a way that states receive

[35] S.D. Brunn and W.L. Hoffman, "The Geography of Federal Grants-in-Aid to States," *Economic Geography*, v. 45, n. 6 (1969).

increased funding from the federal government on the basis of past effectiveness in eliminating poverty within their borders.[36]

In his later article exploring the AFDC program, Wohlenberg sets out to analyze the gross inequalities in welfare standards and benefits in the United States. He discovers that each state has prepared and published a list of standards to measure individual need for welfare assistance, and that the interpretation and application of standards is somewhat dependent on the individual decisions of the caseworkers. Wohlenberg also discovers two separate factors impinging on funding levels. The first is bureaucratic inertia, which refers to the funding agency's slowness to modify rules and regulations to enable more or fewer needy people to receive aid as economic conditions fluctuate. The second is the reluctance of the needy to seek aid, either because of the social stigma attached to being a welfare recipient, or because of the lack of sophistication required to apply for grants.[37]

Other geographers have focused on the state as supplier outside the context of federal grant programs. Green posits five types of service provision to individuals and families: (1) self help (including family help), (2) mutual aid (involving the concept of reciprocity), (3) philanthropy, (4) commercial provision, and (5) government provision. Each time a service is delivered—regardless of the type of service—the delivery may be more or less effective, depending upon three factors: (1) the level of motivation of the controllers of the service, (2) the degree of motivation of the service deliverer, and (3) the unintended consequences of participants' actions.[38]

Jones and Kirby discuss the "geography of consumption." They believe that the distribution of public resources is not important as an issue in and of itself, but that it should be viewed instead as an important link between the individual and the operation of the state.[39] The authors' linkage of the role of the state as supplier with a more general theory of the state is a rarity within the literature, and Jones and Kirby are to be praised for their insight. Clarke and Prentice develop various mathematical models of resource allocation while contributing little to the advancement of theory in this area.[40]

---

[36] E.H. Wohlenberg, "Public Assistance Effectiveness by States," *Annals of the Association of American Geographers*, v. 66, n. 3 (1976).

[37] E.H. Wohlenberg, "Interstate Variations in AFDC Programs," *Economic Geography*, v. 52, n. 3 (1979).

[38] Green, "The Spatial Sciences and the State".

[39] K. Jones and A. Kirby, "Provision and Well-Being: An Agenda for Public Resources Research," *Environment and Planning-A*, v. 14, n. 3 (1982).

[40] M. Clarke and R. Prentice, "Exploring Decisions in Public Policy-Making: Strategic Allocation, Individual Allocation and Simulation, " *Environment and Planning-A*, v. 14, n. 3 (1982).

Bohland and Gist view the resource allocation problem from the perspective of politics and bureaucratic decision-making. These two factors, say the authors, are important in the development of regional variation in federal outlays. Specifically, they discuss the interplay between politics and bureaucratic risk-aversion. They predict that projects perceived by the bureaucracy as low-risk ventures will be funded without the necessity of political pressure on the bureaucrats. Conversely, they predict that if a project is perceived by the bureaucrat as high-risk, congressional influence might be required to secure funding approval.[41] One of the most important volumes describing the role of the state as supplier is R.J. Bennett's *The Geography of Public Finance*. In his book, the author defines the geography of public finance as the provision of public services in different locations emphasizing the imbalance between, on the one hand, the spatial pattern of revenue raising and tax exporting, and on the other hand, the geographical distribution of public expenditure benefits. The book therefore is concerned with the issue of equity, that is, equal treatment of equals regardless of location.[42] This book attracted some praise for its innovation in addressing the geographical issues surrounding public finance. Still, there are criticisms. Clark criticized Bennett on two counts. The first stems from Bennett's omission of the issue of political conflict over the actual structure and functions of the government. The second arises because of Bennett's idealized model of the state, which specifies that the state is only a producer, supplying goods to its citizen consumers.[43] This continuing emphasis on the economic aspects of the role of the state is, as we have seen, a traditional approach that warrants attention.

By and large, the geographical literature on the role of the state as supplier is practical in nature. There is little underlying theory linking the research in this field. Yet the issue of autonomy provides a larger framework within the study of geography and the state that geographers studying the role of state as supplier may find useful as a means of linking this research. Perhaps as the field grows, a greater degree of integration will occur.

The State as Regulator

The state has acted as a regulator since its inception: each prohibition and each law may be viewed as a form of regulation. In recent years, the growing role of the state as regulator has more or less coincided with the growing interest of the new public administration in such issues as citizen

---

[41] J.R. Bohland and J. Gist, "The Spatial Consequences of Bureaucratic Decision-Making," *Environment and Planning-A*, v. 15, n. 11 (November 1983).

[42] Bennett, *The Geography of Public Finance*.

[43] G.L. Clark, Review of *The Geography of Public Finance*, by R.J. Bennett, *Progress in Human Geography*, v. 6, n. 4 (1983).

participation, client control, and value consciousness. Indeed, many regulations resulted from citizen activism in the sixties and early seventies. For example, the National Environmental Policy Act of 1969 followed several years of demonstrations and political efforts by environmental groups in the United States. Even before that, civil rights legislation came only after many years of peaceful demonstrations and, ultimately, several major riots. It is clear, then, that within the role of the state as regulator, we should begin to seek linkages between citizens and government activity. However, the geographical approach tends to look at the effects of the regulation rather than at the linkages within the chain of regulation, as we will see.

Urban policy has long been of interest to geographers. Clark reported on the basic elements of President Carter's Urban Impact Analysis (UIA) initiative and commented on the relevance of this policy as a tool for geographical research and urban policy analysis. The UIA initiative required that all government actions be evaluated before implementation with respect to potential impacts on the urban environment. To the extent possible, it required that the actions be modified if necessary so that implementation would be consistent with overall U.S. urban policy.

There were three major premises underlying the implementation of the UIA, says Clark. First, the public sector plays a major role in the growth and decline of the total urban system through its many policy initiatives. Second, the major effects of federal policies on urban areas are not necessarily exclusively the result of policies originating within agencies having an explicit urban mandate or mission, such as HUD. Finally, by targeting UIA to federal policies, the government acknowledges that in spite of all its efforts, it may fail to identify all the consequences of its actions.[44]

Clark notes that UIA was important both because it reflected a concern on the part of the federal government over the bureaucratic nature of policy decision-making and because it marked a subtle shift of responsibility for urban problems from the private sector to the public sector. In addition, Clark seems to believe that the implementation of UIA implies that "big government" has agreed to shoulder at least some of the blame for urban problems.

In a later article, Clark, along with Gertler, discusses U.S. policies regarding local labor markets during the 1970s with respect to their target efficiency and their underlying theoretical assumptions. The authors find that the policies of the Economic Development Administration (EDA) are target inefficient when compared to those of the Comprehensive Employment and Training Act (CETA), and they identify two types of inefficiency. Vertical inefficiency occurs when a program intended to benefit a particular

---

[44] G.L. Clark, "Urban Impact Analysis: A New Tool for Monitoring the Geographical Effects of Federal Policies," *Professional Geographer*, v. 32, n. 1 (January 1980).

low-income group also benefits another, higher income group. Horizontal inefficiency occurs when a program fails to reach all the members of the designated target group.[45]

Ross also discusses U.S. labor policy, although his major emphasis is on "global capitalism." Ross expresses an interest in three basic types of policy: (1) policy that affects the reproduction of labor, (2) policy that tries to attract private capital through subsidies, and (3) tax policy and incentives. Ross's findings indicate that public policies that attempt to direct the localization of jobs through federal inducements are probably less successful than public policy that mediates labor-capital relations in achieving their purposes.[46]

Storper, Walker, and Widess studied the firm's response to public regulations. Their findings indicate that contrary to conventional assumptions, industry seems not to consider the impacts of local regulations until after selecting a site on the basis of economic factors. Rather, the firm assumes that regulations are not a significant impediment since most cities are eager to attract new business and are often willing to relax local ordinances to achieve this objective. The authors also acknowledge that the letter of the law is not always the effect of the law, given the role of local politics in policy implementation.[47]

Turning to another aspect of U.S. regulatory policy, taxation, opens a fertile field. Smith and Shapiro discuss the effects of the passage of the California Property Tax Limitation Amendment in 1978. The primary effect of this act was to increase the relative importance of the state sales tax as a source of government revenues. In turn, the authors predict spatial inequalities in tax dollar flows.[48]

Thrall has done a considerable amount of work in the area of tax assessment. In a 1979 article, he identifies a method of mapping the classic economic public goods into a spatial realm. In this work, Thrall theorizes that residents of the central business district have a greater preference for public goods than do inhabitants of fringe areas, because with increasing density, there is an increasing need to control externalities. This control comes by way of increased public services.[49]

---

[45] G.L. Clark and M. Gertler, "Local Labor Markets: Theories and Policies in the United States during the 1970s," *Professional Geographer*, v. 35, n. 3 (August 1983).

[46] R.J.S. Ross, "Facing Leviathan: Public Policy and Global Capitalism," *Economic Geography*, v. 59, n. 2 (April 1983).

[47] M. Storper, R. Walker, and B. Widess, "Performance Regulation and Industrial Location: A Case Study," *Environment and Planning-A*, v. 13, n. 3 (March 1981).

[48] P. Shapiro and T.R. Smith, "Public Policy Assessment: Evaluating Objectives of Resource Policies," *Economic Geography*, v. 55, n. 2 (April 1979).

[49] G.I. Thrall, "Public Goods and the Derivation of Land Value Assessment Schedule within a Spatial Equilibrium Setting," *Geographical Analysis*, v. 11, n. 1 (January 1979).

In another 1979 article, Thrall describes a framework for identifying and evaluating the existence and causes of property tax inequities resulting from incorrect assessments. Taking empirical evidence from Canada, Thrall discovers that very low-priced houses were slightly overtaxed, while high-priced houses were significantly undertaxed. Midpriced houses, he finds, were generally reasonably assessed.[50]

In a 1981 article, "Dynamics in the Structural Form of Property Taxes," Thrall begins with the premise that the purpose of the property tax is to divide the local public sector's costs among the various types of land users. Because the property tax is structurally tied to the market value of houses through the assessment function, he says, rapid increases in the market values of houses will lead to increases in local property taxes. Thrall recommends that property tax millage rates be indexed to counterbalance changes in market values.[51]

One of the areas where the state has traditionally acted as regulator is in the area of energy policy. In the United States, the federal government has consistently played a role in the availability and pricing of energy, actually setting prices, requiring energy producers to institute safety and evacuation measures, and in other indirect ways as well. It is therefore useful to review the work that geographers have done in the general area of energy regulation by the state.

Two authors have examined the relationship between the United States federal government and energy. Beard discusses the impact of federal environmental regulations on energy resources, focusing on the Clean Air Act Amendments of 1970, the Federal Water Pollution Control Act Amendments of 1972, the National Environmental Policy Act of 1969, and the Coastal Zone Management Act of 1972.[52] He finds that conflicts arose between these regulations and energy resources in several areas. First, land-use conflicts became a problem, especially where exploitable energy resources lay underneath environmentally significant and sensitive areas. Second, fuel-switching posed a problem, particularly where clean-air regulations forced an end to the use of cheaper, locally found, high-sulfur coal in the midwestern and eastern parts of the United States. Finally, problems arose over changes in production and transportation technologies. How much would these changes add to the cost of fuels? How safe and effective

---

[50] G.I. Thrall, "Spatial Inequities in Tax Assessment: A Case Study of Hamilton, Ontario," *Economic Geography*, v. 55, n. 2 (April 1979).

[51] G.I. Thrall, "Dynamics in the Structural Form of Property Taxes," *Professional Geographer*, v. 33, n. 4 (April 1981).

[52] D.P. Beard, "United States Environmental Legislation and Energy Resources: A Review," *Geographical Review*, v. 65, n. 2 (April 1975): 229-44.

would these technologies be? Beard identifies these problems but offers no solutions.

In a later article, Osleeb evaluates the Strategic Petroleum Reserve (SPR) program of the U.S. Department of Energy (DOE).[53] The SPR requires that the DOE plan, accumulate, store, and maintain a supply of crude oil and petroleum products to be used in case of an interruption in crude oil supplies to the United States. Using a linear programming model to evaluate the program, Osleeb concludes that the plan is generally well formulated, and that the stockpile should help significantly if the U.S. oil supply is cut. Still, only an actual emergency will provide a definitive answer to the question of how large the stockpile should be.

Haynes, Phillips, and Solomon describe a model for planning the distribution of coal-fired power plants in the presence of environmental constraints.[54] Their model is particularly sensitive to the economic parameters of the coal industry's environment. The authors' model includes such factors as the absolute cost of facility construction, the availability of capital, and the economic costs of environmental and other regulatory legislation. It should be noted that this model was developed for the benefit of the coal industry and thus has a predominantly economic orientation.

Pijawka and Chalmers explore the impacts of a nuclear generating facility on a local community.[55] Their analysis, too, focuses on the economic impacts, but they recognize that local groups of activists can play a role in the location of a nuclear facility. The authors note that decision-makers are beginning to understand the importance of anticipating public response to major public works projects. Pijawka and Chalmers discover that the location of nuclear facilities does not bring significant economic benefits to the communities in which they are located, largely because construction is often subcontracted to specialized, nonlocal firms. Neither does the completed facility act as an incentive for new industry to locate in the area if there are no other incentives.

Another pair of authors, Semple and Richetto, characterize the nuclear power plant as an experimental public facility and discuss the trends in its adoption and location.[56] The authors use what is basically a product-cycle curve to characterize the phases in the development of nuclear power. The

[53] J.P. Osleeb, "An Evaluation of the Strategic Petroleum Reserve Program of the U.S. Department of Energy," *Professional Geographer*, v. 31, n. 4 (November 1979): 393-99.

[54] K.E. Haynes, F.Y. Phillips, and B.D. Solomon, "A Coal Industry Distribution Planning Model under Environmental Constraints," *Economic Geography*, v. 59, n. 1 (January 1983).

[55] D. Pijawka and J. Chalmers, "Impacts of Nuclear Generating Plants on Local Areas," *Economic Geography*, v. 59, n. 1 (January 1983): 66-80.

[56] R.K. Semple and J.P. Richetto, "Locational Trends of an Experimental Public Facility: The Case of Nuclear Power Plants," *Professional Geographer*, v. 28, n. 3 (August 1976): 248-53.

first phase is experimental, during which a few pilot facilities are located near traditional facilities with accepted technologies. During the second stage, there is a period of rapid expansion of the innovation, which exhibits a bandwagon effect. Phase three is a period of retrenchment. Because of the rapid expansion occurring in the second phase (and possible resulting problems), a wait-and-see attitude develops. New environmental safeguards, stricter public regulations, and private user rationalization may occur before more complete adoption of the technology becomes feasible. Phase four is a second period of expansion, occurring at a more controlled rate. It would appear that the U.S. nuclear industry is currently stalled in phase three, largely as a result of the accident at Three Mile Island, an accident the authors could not have anticipated when they published their article in 1976. It is probable that the 1986 accident at Chernobyl in the Soviet Union will be an additional barrier to the nuclear industry as it seeks to reach phase four.

The incident at Three Mile Island (TMI) precipitated a flurry of articles in the geographical literature on evacuation behavior. Zeigler, Johnson, and Brunn—in various combinations and permutations—have written several articles on the subject, as have Cutter and Barnes.[57]

Zeigler and Johnson discover that public response to the Pennsylvania governor's limited evacuation advisory reflected a decided over-response among people residing in the vicinity of Three Mile Island.[58] By contrast, earlier evacuation studies, which had natural disaster as the cause of evacuation, indicated that affected residents exhibited a marked under-response to evacuation advisories.

Zeigler and Johnson's study corroborates an earlier study by Zeigler, Brunn, and Johnson in which the authors describe what they call the "evacuation shadow phenomenon,"[59] that is, the tendency of an official evacuation advisory to cause departure from a much larger area than was intended. The authors also found that in addition to the tendency for more people to flee than intended, people tend to flee from greater distances in relation to the nuclear disaster site than for natural disasters.

Johnson and Zeigler, in yet another article, discuss human behavior in a nuclear disaster as it relates to new federal evacuation regulations.[60] The new regulations assume that people will follow evacuation orders, in

---

[57] S. Cutter and K. Barnes, "Evacuation Behavior and Three Mile Island," *Disasters*, v. 6 (1982): 116-24.

[58] D. Zeigler and J.H. Johnson, Jr., "Evacuation Behavior in Response to Nuclear Power Plant Accidents," *Professional Geographer*, v. 36, n. 2 (1984): 207-15.

[59] D. Zeigler, S.D. Brunn, and J.H. Johnson, Jr., "Evacuation from a Nuclear Technological Disaster," *Geographical Review*, v. 71 (1981): 1-16.

[60] J.H. Johnson, Jr., and D. Zeigler, "Distinguishing Human Response to Radiological Emergencies," *Economic Geography*, v. 59, pp. 386-402.

spite of empirical evidence to the contrary. Although some people will underreact, most will overreact and create havoc in evacuation plans. The authors suggest that emergency planners accept the fact that human behavior cannot be controlled, and try to capitalize on that behavior as they develop evacuation plans. The authors offer no suggestions about how this can be done and admit their failure.[61]

Most closely related to this paper is Mercer's discussion of the location of a high-voltage line in Australia.[62] Mercer discusses the conflict between the power company, which enjoyed the backing of the government, and local conservation groups who fought their battle alone and with limited resources. Faced with such a powerful opponent, the conservationists could only fail. Mercer's article is important to this research because it begins to make the connection between the relative power of participants in the decision-making process, and the decision itself. The article is also important for what it lacks: an emphasis on economics.

The emphasis in the literature on the state's role as regulator, as we have seen, is generally limited to the outcomes of federal regulations. The link between citizen participation and regulation is largely ignored. Furthermore, there is no mention of the role of clients. In light of the growing interest in the literature of collective action and its role in government, geographers would do well to explore this side of the question as well.

The State as Social Engineer

The role of the state as social engineer brings us once again to the issue of autonomy. That the state is in the business of social engineering presumes that the state has goals. Those goals are rarely without implications for other units of government. For example, the abolition of slavery caused great economic hardship in the South and sent repercussions that echoed for many years throughout the nation. Because of the potentially great ramifications of federal social engineering efforts, such efforts merit serious study. Yet, in general, the geographic literature tends toward an economic approach, often at the expense of social justice considerations.

Thrall has made an interesting contribution to the literature on the state as social engineer. In a 1978 article, he and Casetti discuss an ideal urban center wherein the rules of interaction between local government and

---

61 This article is corroborated in my personal experience by a former colleague who had previously worked for the Illinois Emergency Services and Disaster Agency (ESDA). He described the evacuation plan for the Dresden Plant near Chicago, then added that, given the panic factor (or the evacuation shadow phenomenon, as Ziegler et al. call it), a great many people would perish in a real disaster, in spite of the best-laid plans of ESDA.

62 D. Mercer, "Conflict over a High Voltage Power Line: A Victoria Case Study," *Australian Geographer*, v. 15, n. 5 (May 1983): 292-307.

citizens allow the citizens to make choices regarding local public goods. This system is designed so that public goods are valued by and defined as the number of hours worked by the producers of public goods per unit of residential land consumed by the household. Citizens decide how many units of goods they want at a given price, rather than being taxed. The government, according to the model, is constrained to have a balanced budget.[63]

An important and oft repeated concept in social engineering is the concept of efficiency. Yet there is little agreement on what constitutes efficiency. Massam, for whom efficiency has a strictly economic meaning, provides an in-depth discussion of how geographers could locate facilities for maximum economic efficiency.[64] Although the author does well to introduce the idea that the form of administration is a matter of some importance to policy outcomes, he tries too hard to formulate his ideas into quantitative economic theory. The outcome is that his work turns out to be little more than a literature review of failed organizational models.

Williams admits that efficiency is a slippery concept, remaining largely unexplored in terms of for whom or for what; yet he notes that a great deal of attention has been directed to the search for organizational arrangements that will optimize efficiency. The author believes that in the quest for efficiency researchers have lost sight of more important questions. Williams makes the basic point that in light of the ability of organizations to influence policy outcomes, they warrant more careful attention than they have received thus far.[65]

Another elusive concept, often used as an alternative to efficiency, is that of equity. The federal government has developed and implemented many programs to promote equity among its citizens and thus to perform its role as social engineer. Hoggart studies federal outlays in a geographic region composed of the states of Illinois, Indiana, Michigan, Ohio, and Wisconsin. His findings indicate that in general, total outlays in the region are poorly related to social needs. Outlays from two departments (Agriculture; and Health, Education and Welfare), however, are closely related to need. Hoggart also finds that political representation has little impact on the distribution of Agriculture and HEW grants in the study area.[66]

---

[63] G.I. Thrall and E. Casetti, "Local Public Goods and Spatial Equilibrium in an Ideal Urban Center," *Canadian Geographer*, v. 22 (Winter 1978).

[64] B. Massam, *Location and Space in Social Administration* (New York: John Wiley and Sons, 1975).

[65] P. Williams, "Restructuring Urban Managerialism: Towards a Political Economy of Urban Allocation," *Environment and Planning-A*, v. 14, n. 1 (January 1982).

[66] K. Hoggart, "Social Needs, Political Representation, and Federal Outlays in the East North Central United States of America," *Environment and Planning-A*, v. 13, n. 5 (May 1981).

Related to the question of equity is the issue of geographical differences in economic development. Adams says that several ingredients contribute to regional concentrations of high vitality, including the redistribution of income through federal tax and expenditure policies. He goes on to discuss the migration of individuals within neighborhoods and between regions. He notes that in general, each move made by an individual or family is in the upward direction to a better neighborhood or to a city that is economically healthier.[67]

Fuchs and Demko discuss geographic inequality in the context of a socialist system, noting that in the Soviet Union and northeastern Europe, there are marked inequalities along three different scales: (1) urban-rural, (2) interurban, and (3) intraurban. Explanations, like the disparities themselves, are not limited to their economic setting, but can be applied to a capitalist or mixed system as well as to a socialist setting. The explanations include the following: historical disparities; the favoring of efficiency over equity; the favoring of investment in productive sectors as opposed to infrastructure investment; the growing scale requirement of service and human welfare facilities; and inequalities in income distribution.[68]

Local governments have also undertaken social engineering activities, and geographers have commented. Burns discusses the financial analysis of various alternatives to suburban annexation, noting that whereas in the past, annexation was presumed to be cost-effective, this is not the case today. Nowadays, the cost of providing public services to the annexed area may outweigh the tax benefits of adding new territory to the town.[69]

Wolch and Gabriel discuss local land development policies and their effects on urban housing values. Their research suggests that local governments have multiple objectives and constraints that shape their policy stance toward growth. The authors' findings also indicate that local land-use policies have important effects on housing prices. Restrictive policies, they find, increase average home values by about 15 percent.[70]

Just as policymaking and implementation are important issues, so too is policy evaluation. Smit and Johnston describe a type of policy evalu-

---

[67] J.S. Adams, "A Geographical Basis for Urban Public Policy," *Professional Geographer*, v. 31, n. 2 (February 1979).

[68] R. Fuchs and G. Demko, "Geographic Inequality under Socialism," *Annals of the Association of American Geographers*, v. 69, n. 2 (June 1979).

[69] E.K. Burns, "Financial Analysis of Suburban Annexation Alternatives," *Professional Geographer*, v. 33, n. 2 (February 1981).

[70] J.R. Wolch and S.A. Gabriel, "Local Land Development Policies and Urban Housing Values," *Environment and Planning-A*, v. 13, n. 10 (October 1981).

ation in which policy objectives are assessed relative to perceived resource use and resource policy problems.[71]

Public location questions constitute a special type of social engineering by the state that is particularly relevant to the Bailly case. In the late 1960s, geographers began to turn their attention to the siting of public facilities, an issue more often than not a matter of public controversy. In the case of desirable public facilities, such as military bases (which can bring considerable revenue-generating capacity to a region) or housing for the elderly (which potential neighbors may perceive as bringing nice, quiet neighbors next door), communities will compete with one another to attract federal investment. In the case of undesirable public facilities, such as prisons (which will locate known felons nearby), or low-income housing (which potential neighbors may view as enabling "low-life" welfare recipients to live side by side with upstanding members of the community), neighborhoods and cities fight tooth-and-nail to repel government intervention. The geographic implications are clear, and there is a good deal of literature on the subject, of which I present a small sample.

An important early study of public location theory is Teitz's "Toward a Theory of Urban Public Facility Location."[72] In this article, Teitz shows an acute awareness of the basic differences between the public and private sectors and an appreciation for specifically public location problems such as the social welfare function of the state and the absence of a competitive pricing system in the public sector. Teitz notes that the government produces goods and services that vary along two separate dimensions: the individual choice of consumers and the pricing of goods. Individual choice refers to the citizen's ability to choose to receive a government good. For example, we cannot choose to refuse certain goods such as police protection or national defense. The government provides these services over a specific jurisdiction and all who live within that jurisdiction are protected. Citizens can decline to accept other services, such as libraries or parks, simply by staying away.

The second dimension, the pricing of goods, refers to costs associated with using a public good, including fee-for-use and travel costs. For example, we do not pay for national defense on a fee-for-use basis. Rather, national defense is included in the cover charge of taxes. On the other hand, we may be charged a user's fee to buy a season's pass at the local public swimming pool. Even some so-called free services (like libraries) involve costs in terms of both time and money required to get to the source of the

---

[71] B. Smit and R.J. Johnston, "Public Policy Assessment: Evaluating Objectives of Resource Policies," *Professional Geographer*, v. 35, n. 2 (February 1983).

[72] M.B. Teitz, "Toward a Theory of Urban Public Facility Location," *Papers, Regional Science Association*, v. 21 (1968 [Cambridge meeting, November 1967]): 35-52.

good. Teitz's model sets out to consider those public/private sector differences and he appeals for a field of location theory specifically devoted to urban public facilities. This work is important for its distinctively and astutely public approach to public location.

Echoing Teitz, Dear also shows a keen understanding of the unique problems and ramifications of public location.[73] Dear contends that indeed we must understand public sector location because of the significant role of public facility location as the primary generator of land-use change. These changes, he says, elicit private sector responses. Dear, too, takes the position that tinkering with private location models will not necessarily yield valid public sector models. He cites as the basis of his argument the fact that redistribution of income is a crucial element in any public policy decision.

Dear also brings up the issue of conflict over public facility location that is so often a part of the decision. In addition, he discusses both direct and indirect effects of public location decisions. Direct effects are those affecting the consumers of a facility, whereas indirect effects affect non-consumers as well. For example, the direct effect of building a prison in Hyde Park on Chicago's South Side would be that more Chicago-area people convicted of a crime could live near their homes and families. The indirect effect would probably be the relocation of Hyde Parkers capable of moving to other areas where they could avoid this new neighbor. It is not only the direct effects that have the capacity to generate conflict, but the indirect effects as well.

Moore discussed the impacts of a major medical center on income in the region in which the center was built, and discovered that large public institutions have the capacity to generate millions of dollars in personal income and employment.[74] Several other geographers, notably Dear,[75], Mercer and Hultquist,[76] and Wolch and Gabriel[77] have discussed the siting of mental health care facilities and public low-income housing, both of which are usually considered to be undesirable additions to a neighborhood.

In spite of the best efforts of both Teitz and Dear to spread the word that public location is different from private location, their works seem to have spawned a series of mathematical models of public facility location that are little more than warmed-over versions of private facility location

[73] Dear, "A Paradigm for Public Facility Location Theory," pp. 46-50.

[74] C.L. Moore, "The Impact of Public Institutions on Regional Income, Upstate Medical Center as a Case in Point," *Economic Geography*, v. 50, n. 2 (April 1974).

[75] Dear, "A Paradigm for Public Facility Location Theory"; and idem, "Locational Factors in the Demand for Mental Health Care," *Economic Geography*, v. 53, n. 3 (March 1977).

[76] J. Mercer and J. Hultquist, "National Progress Toward Housing and Urban Renewal Goals," in *Urban Policymaking and Metropolitan Dynamics: A Comparative Geographical Analysis*, ed. John S. Adams (Cambridge, Mass.: Ballinger, 1976).

[77] Wolch and Gabriel, "Local Land Development Policies and Urban Housing Values."

models. These models share one element in common: a quest to find the "least cost solution." Papers by ReVelle and Swain,[78] Rojeski and ReVelle,[79] Wagner and Falkson,[80] and Hodgson[81] fall into this category. Because these works neglect the important differences between public and private location decisions, they add little to the geographical literature on public facility location. For this reason, I will say no more about them.

Another part of the literature makes a very important contribution by alerting geographers to the public sector need to weigh economic concerns against equity needs. This contribution relates to Teitz's concern with social welfare as well as to Dear's concern with redistribution.

The first of these articles is by Mumphrey and Wolpert, who point out that there is an inherent conflict between economic efficiency and equity and that these two factors function as mutual constraints.[82] The authors note that the equity needs of groups and individuals are adversely affected by public projects, especially if the individuals in question possess meager political resources. More powerful groups—those who have the resources to halt or delay the proposed project—may in later projects be brought into the process at an earlier stage to avert problems by arranging mitigating features or otherwise fostering compromise.

Morrill discusses distance to a service as it relates to equity concerns.[83] The author notes that many public location models yield solutions that locate public facilities in the densest areas without regard to the need for public facilities among people in more sparsely settled areas. Morrill believes that such solutions should not be automatically accepted, and that in some cases it may be more equitable—and in some circumstances more economical—to provide some sort of compensatory services to those with poor access.

Hodge and Gatrell assert that the arrangement of residential areas of various social groups is a major cause of inequality of access to public facili-

[78] C.S. ReVelle and R.W. Swain, "Central Facilities Location," *Geographical Analysis*, v. 2 (1970): 30-42.

[79] P. Rojeski and C.S. ReVelle, "Central Facilities Location under an Investment Constraint," *Geographical Analysis*, v. 2 (1970): 343-60.

[80] J.L. Wagner and L.M. Falkson, "The Optimal Nodal Location of Public Facilities with Price-Sensitive Demand," *Geographical Analysis*, v. 7 (1975): 69-83.

[81] M.J. Hodgson, "Toward a More Realistic Allocation in Location-Allocation Models: An Interaction Approach," *Environment and Planning-A*, v. 10 (1978): 1273-85.

[82] A.J. Mumphrey and J. Wolpert, "Equity Considerations and Concessions in the Siting of Public Facilities," *Economic Geography*, v. 94 (1973): 104-21.

[83] R.L. Morrill, "Efficiency and Equity of Optimum Location Models," *Antipode*, v. 6 (1974): 41-46.

ties.[84] The authors argue that the range of a facility has a significant impact on the distribution of benefits among the various social classes. As the range increases, the number of people within the service area increases; therefore, the probability of each social group being served equally increases. This article seems to argue for centralization of public facilities, as has been done in the case of consolidation of schools in rural areas, as a strategy to overcome inequality in access to facilities. Although the authors' idea to centralize facilities would permit access to people who might otherwise be kept out, it fails to consider the cost of travel to those far away.

McAllister argues that in weighing efficiency against equity, there is no objective answer. But, he says, equity is far more sensitive to the size and spacing of facilities than is efficiency.[85] His results suggest that equity as a prime criterion is very important in the design of public service systems and therefore deserves more attention than it has received to date.

Hodgart contends that the final decisions about the location of all public facilities are political.[86] He goes on to defend mathematical models on the grounds that they can show that some solutions are better than others based on objective measures, arguing that such models can weigh different combinations of equity and efficiency, and thus aid decision-makers. Although Hodgart recognizes the inherent conflict between efficiency and equity, his analysis underestimates the complexity of equity considerations.

A third group of authors, Murray, Smith, and Wolpert, introduce the use of the phrase "noxious public facilities."[87] The authors discuss here a situation wherein a needed but noxious facility is being sited in the face of inevitable opposition. They recommend that the decision-makers be prepared to provide some sort of compensation to those most affected by the facility, especially if those who are affected have the capacity to halt or delay construction and thus to add substantially to construction costs. The authors suggest that decision-makers attempt to develop models, such as theirs, that build in an opposition factor, including both the probability of any particular group offering opposition and the cost of that opposition. At the same time, they recognize the difficulty of accurately modeling such a complex variable.

---

[84] D. Hodge and A. Gatrell, "Spatial Constraints and the Location of Urban Public Facilities," *Environment and Planning-A*, (1976): 215-30.

[85] D.M. McAllister, "Equity and Efficiency in Public Facility Location," *Geographical Analysis*, v. 8 (1976): 47-63.

[86] R.L. Hodgart, "Optimizing Access to Public Services: A Review of Problems, Models, and Methods of Locating Central Facilities," *Progress in Human Geography*, n. 2 (1978): 17-48.

[87] M. Austin, T. Smith, and J. Wolpert, "The Implementation of Controversial Facility-Complex Programs," *Geographical Analysis*, v. 2 (1970): 315-29.

Papageorgiou agrees with Murray, Smith, and Wolpert that models should take into consideration the costs of compensating groups and individuals for the siting of noxious facilities.[88] He develops such a model, based on the notion that the marginal social costs of a facility should equal its marginal social benefits. Where such a situation occurs, that point represents the optimum siting decision.

Papageorgiou brings to the literature the term "externality," which refers to the negative side effects (much like the "indirect effects" as defined by Dear) of a public facility.

Dear, Taylor, and Hall also discuss externalities.[89] They observe that in spite of recent attempts to clarify the theoretical bases of spatial externalities, little is known about their incidence in the real world. They note further that the response of those affected by externalities is barely mentioned. The authors posit a chain of events wherein externalities cause negative effects which, in turn, cause conflict. Conflict, in its turn, precipitates an extended sequence of political decision-making. The authors suggest that geographers should study real-life situations in order to determine whether the causal chain they developed is plausible. Dear and Taylor followed their own suggestion and two years later published a book exploring the link between externalities and location decisions, and discussing local attitudes toward mental health facilities.[90] Their findings indicate that their earlier hypothesized causal chain is accurate. To a large extent, this research also examines that causal chain.

The work thus far undertaken by geographers in the siting of public facilities is not overwhelming.[91] But the literature does show an appreciation for the special problems and conditions prevalent in the public sector. Slowly, geographers are moving away from models based almost exclusively on economic concerns to include more complex, equity-related factors.

The discussion of the state's role as social engineer tends to concentrate on engineering to the detriment of the social aspect. This concentration has given the discussion an overwhelmingly economic approach that neglects McNee's call for geographers to become social critics.[92] In fact, by

---

[88] G.J. Papageorgiou, "Spatial Externalities: Parts I and II," *Annals of the Association of American Geographers*, v. 68 (1978): 465-92.

[89] M.J. Dear, M. Taylor, and G.B. Hall, "External Effects of Mental Health Facilities," *Annals of the Association of American Geographers*, v. 70, n. 3 (1980): 342-52.

[90] M.J. Dear and M. Taylor, *Not on Our Street: Community Attitudes toward Mental Health Care* (London: Pion, 1982).

[91] I should mention here that I have intentionally omitted a body of location literature that deals specifically with the siting problems unique to public mental health care facilities. It is a highly specialized literature, and not directly applicable to the more general topic of public facility location.

[92] McNee, "Regional Planning, Bureaucracy, and Geography," p. 192.

and large, the literature of geography and the state is almost entirely descriptive and, until recent years, devoid of social criticism. One may argue that social criticism is not the geographer's role, that we should be objective academics. Indeed, debate over objectivity and bias-free research has been carried out over many years by many philosophers both within and outside the discipline. This philosophical issue certainly will not be resolved here. Suffice it to say, if one accepts McNee's premise, one will find the literature of geography and the state lacking.

Critique of the Literature on the Geography of the State

The geographical literature of the state is not a large body, nor is it particularly well linked in a systematic way. On the whole, the literature is not especially theoretical, but tends to be practice oriented. Still, it is important to know what has come before in order to situate the current research within the existing framework. It would be wishful thinking to say that there is currently a well-defined geography of the state. With a few exceptions, the body of literature described herein fails as a coherent field on several counts.

First and foremost, there seems to be no underlying theory—or even a concerted effort to develop such a theory (or theories) of geography and the state. Rather, most literature seems to address a single issue without being related to any unified body of theory. It is important to note that we are not discussing here the existence of competing or poorly developed theories, but the absence of any unified theory whatsoever. This eclecticism is a serious deficiency and it is beginning to be rectified by the work of Clark, Dear, Bennett, and Johnston. This is not to say that there is agreement on theory among these authors. In fact, the debate is growing more lively and it is possible (and desirable) that others will enter the fray.

Related to the issue of eclecticism is the problem of functionalism. In large part, the literature focuses on the functions of the state. Many of the articles included in my survey of the literature discuss the manner in which a single function was carried out by a particular agency of a specific government. These discussions very often ignore entirely the underlying structure that influences those activities. Again, Clark and Dear have led the way in providing an understanding of form, which work can pave the way for development of a theory of the state.

The literature on geography and the state has fallen short in another important way. Although the literature has focused largely on issues in the public sector, the serious differences between the public and private sectors have been neglected. Geographers have treated public sector issues as they treated private sector issues—from a largely economic point of view, even though the differences are significant and have important ramifications.

Dear stands apart in his clear understanding of these differences and his admonishment to geographers to reflect them in their research was forceful; it is surprising that geographical literature on public policy issues continues to neglect Dear's advice. Inasmuch as the great proportion of the literature described in this paper makes no distinction between the economics of the public and private sectors, it is seriously flawed. Once again, a few geographers are beginning to write about the public sector from a more enlightened perspective, but more is needed.

State Apparatus: Bureaucracy

Clark and Dear's *State Apparatus* represents an effort to bring together the diverse themes in the literature of geography and the state into a unified theory. Essentially, *State Apparatus* provides a theoretical perspective on the state from a Weberian perspective aimed at understanding the spatial organization of the state as an organization. Thus, the authors establish the basic link between state form and function, although their work does not discuss the specific nature of that state apparatus. *State Apparatus* makes several important points that warrant discussion.

First, Clark and Dear argue that "rather than designing the state as an agent of the status quo, it is possible to think of a positive, goal-oriented state."[93] It is true that in certain cases, one can identify state goals. The U.S. commitment in the sixties to an expansion of civil rights and economic benefits to classes of people who had previously been left out is an example. The commitment in the seventies to environmental concerns is another. However, it is often difficult to identify specific, consistent state goals. For example, one of the concerns expressed during the Iran-Contra hearings specifically asked the question, what is the state goal? On the one hand, the U.S. State Department pursued a national policy in the Middle East that favored Iraq against Iran, perceived as an anti–U.S. terrorist. On the other hand, administration staffers sold arms to Iran for use against Iraq. It is possible to think of a positive, goal-oriented state as Dear and Clark argue, but in reality we cannot always clearly identify a state goal. In the case of the Iran-Contra affair, the report of the Tower Commission's investigation points directly to failures in the organizational structure of the Reagan administration as a cause of the controversy.

The very nature of the U.S. political system makes it difficult to agree on what constitute state goals. Do the president's goals automatically constitute the state's goals? President Reagan repeatedly argued this case, basing his claim on what he called an electoral "mandate." However, when we examine his "mandate" more carefully, and account for the fact that

---

[93] G.L. Clark and M.J. Dear, *State Apparatus* (Boston: Allen and Unwin, 1984), p. 194.

roughly half of all eligible voters failed to cast a ballot for any candidate, it becomes clear that Reagan's "mandate" amounts to support from roughly 30 percent of all eligible voters. Clark and Dear themselves mention "the potential for mistaking indifference, or real dissatisfaction, for loyalty,"[94] suggesting that they, too, are aware of the problem of identifying which goals constitute state goals on the basis of election results.

Even at times when the president's goals and the will of the people seem to be in agreement, the nature and timing of the national electoral process in the United States would seem to raise questions about the longevity of state goals. With a four-year presidential cycle, and an eight-year limitation on the length of presidential tenure, state goals in the United States necessarily appear to be rather short-term, especially in terms of implementation of policies designed to achieve such goals. A president who has the opportunity to make a number of significant judicial appointments may continue to cast a shadow after his term of office has ended, but even these effects may be limited.

State Apparatus provides a discussion of presidential appointments, describing how President Reagan's appointment of Clarence Pendleton shifted the focus (and hence the outcomes) of the Justice Department's Civil Rights Division.[95] Although he himself was black, Pendleton implemented policies that muted the efforts of the Civil Rights Division on behalf of minority groups. In this instance, the president succeeded in putting in place an apparatus for furthering his (and therefore the state's) goal of disassembling affirmative action efforts. On the other hand, Reagan had far less success in carrying off a similar feat in his appointment of Dr. C. Everett Koop as surgeon general of the United States. Koop's attitudes on medical questions with moral implications (abortion and birth control, for example) were apparently consistent with Reagan's and there was general public concern early in Koop's term about the effect of his private opinions on public policy. Over time, however, Koop won substantial support from people all along the political spectrum (and especially from the liberal wing) for his outspoken and seemingly unbiased approach to his responsibilities. In a bureaucratic setting, such absence of bias would be called professionalism. (The characteristics of both the bureaucracy and the individual bureaucrat form the basis for the following chapter.)

The president is not the only legitimate source of state goals: at the federal level, Congress, by virtue of its status as lawmaker, is clearly such a source. The policies of other levels of government (state, county, local, and special service district) also constitute legitimate state goals.

---

[94] Ibid., p. 63.

[95] Ibid., p. 58.

Dear and Clark make a convincing argument for the existence and importance of state apparatus. The Justice Department's Civil Rights Division example clearly shows how important the state apparatus can potentially be in furthering state goals. The example of Koop in the surgeon general's office, by contrast, provides empirical evidence that the state (as personified by the president) does not always control its own apparatus.

Therefore, while *State Apparatus* lays an important foundation for this research, it fails to explain outcomes that are inconsistent with identified state goals. I would argue that the bureaucratic structure of state apparatus is at least partially responsible for the outcomes of state policies. Specific characteristics of the bureaucracy and individual bureaucrats enhance the ability of the bureaucratic state apparatus to play a role in outcomes regardless of state goals. The following chapter discusses these characteristics and describes the role they play in shaping public policy outcomes.

Chapter 3

THE ADMINISTRATIVE BUREAUCRACY

As the literature indicates, geographers have attempted to understand the state and how it functions. While they have made good progress in recent years, in part because of the work of Clark, Dear and others, they have yet to discuss the implications of a specific type of state apparatus, the bureaucracy.

The purpose of this chapter is to outline a theoretical framework for state bureaucracy based on Max Weber's theory of bureaucracy. Weberian theory posits that a major source of a bureaucracy's power is its continuing good relationship with its clientele, the people who share an individual objective with the bureaucracy's organizational goal. Weber claims that the relationship between an organization and its client is one of mutual dependency: each needs the other to survive and/or flourish.

Clients gain from the efforts of the organization in their behalf. Similarly, the clients provide legitimacy and a raison d'etre for the organization. Weber's theory of bureaucracy suggests that the organization has a stake in serving its clientele. The rational bureaucracy, then, will seek to respond to the needs of its clients as a means to ensure its own existence.

Two important issues come into play in this discussion of bureaucracy: bureaucratic rationality and the means by which the client transmits its needs and desires to an organization. In addition to his discussion of bureaucracy, Weber has also written at some length on the general themes of both rationality and on the link between organizations and clients. Jurgen Habermas has likewise commented on these themes, in writings considered by many to be an extension of Weberian theory. In addition, Habermas has focused attention on the medium of communication. For these reasons, the related writings of Habermas serve to illuminate Weberian theory, primarily by providing a counterpoint.

As the Bailly case illustrates, however, legal guarantees of access to the administrative courts within public agencies limit an agency's ability to control communications within its jurisdiction. At the same time, they insure a point of entry for clients (and would-be clients) of the organization. Empirical evidence, then, suggests a significant role for clients in organizational decision-making.

Review of the public administration literature on organization-client relationships can provide additional insight into the relationship I explore in the Bailly case study. In general, this body of literature supports the Weberian perspective, while adding detail on the nature of the organization-client relationship. Among other things, we learn that the more powerful the client group, the more powerful the organization. Conversely, a weak client group is unlikely to spawn a powerful organization. This information is of great importance to any attempt to understand the variations in influence among competing client groups.

Weber's Theory of Bureaucracy

Since it was first translated into English in 1946, Max Weber's theory of bureaucracy has become the keystone of organization theory in the United States. Without a solid understanding of this seminal work, it is difficult to place later work on organization theory in its appropriate context. In his theory, Weber describes an 'ideal' type of organization—ideal in the sense of being a model.

Weber recognized bureaucracies as being relatively efficient, eminently enduring forms of organization. In this section, borrowing heavily from Gerth and Mills[1], I lay out the basic elements of Weber's theory of bureaucracy.

Weber describes six basic characteristics that help identify a bureaucracy. First, the bureaucracy operates under the principles of fixed and official functional areas that are generally ordered by rules such as laws or administrative regulations. Second, the bureaucracy adopts the principles of office hierarchy and graded authority. This results in a firmly ordered system in which higher offices supervise lower ones. Third, management of the bureaucracy is based on written documents—the files—which are preserved in their original form. The maintenance of the files requires a staff that includes "scribes." Fourth, office management usually requires thorough and expert training. Fifth, when the office is fully developed, official duties require that the staff members work full-time. Finally, the

---

1   H.H. Gerth, and C. Wright Mills, *From Max Weber: Essays in Sociology* (New York: Oxford University Press, 1946), pp. 196-244.

management of the office follows general rules that are more or less stable, more or less exhaustive, and that can be learned.

The individual bureaucrat within the organization also has distinguishing characteristics. Officeholding is a vocation for the bureaucrat, and his or her personal position within the office accords the bureaucrat social esteem. The bureaucrat is appointed, not elected, to his or her position, and normally holds that position for an indefinite period. The bureaucrat receives pecuniary compensation in the form of a fixed salary, and his or her well-being in old age is guarded by a pension. The hierarchical arrangement of the office affords the bureaucrat the opportunity for advancement and a life-long career.

There are several technical advantages of bureaucratic organization. Weber contends that the "fully developed bureaucratic machine compares with other organizations exactly as does the machine with non-mechanical modes of production."[2] Weber's ideal bureaucracy is characterized by precision, speed, absence of ambiguity, knowledge of the files, continuity, discretion, unity, strict subordination, and reduction of friction as well as of material and personal costs. The bureaucracy is particularly well-suited to situations where the work is technical and specialized. Our modern world, wherein new and improved technical advances in communication, transportation, and information storage and retrieval are highly valued, invites the bureaucracy as a means of handling ever-increasing specialization.

The bureaucracy is designed to discharge its duties according to calculable rules and "without regard to persons."[3] And because the bureaucracy operates according to calculable rules, any person (or group) who takes the time to learn the rules can gain access to the bureaucracy. The bureaucracy, for its part, delivers its services or carries out its tasks impartially. Hence, in the ideal bureaucracy, equal access and equal treatment are the rules. Still, within the limits of those rules, the bureaucracy has some degree of flexibility in carrying out its responsibilities. It is useful to explore that flexibility vis-à-vis the bureaucracy-client relationship in order to help understand locational decision-making.

Each decision made by an organization is based on several implicit and explicit factors. The expert interpretation of the circumstances surrounding the decision is an immediately obvious explicit factor. Perhaps more interesting, while more elusive, are the implicit factors that operate subtly to influence decisions, and which may add bias to the decision-making process.

---

2   Ibid., p. 214.
3   Ibid., p. 215.

Client groups constitute one such factor. In organizations charged with serving as advocates (HUD, for example, is an advocate for the poor, among others), we expect and even demand that the organization act in ways that further the interest of its clients. In a regulatory agency, however, the organization is charged with guarding a more nebulous client, the "public interest."

Within this general category of regulatory agencies, the Nuclear Regulatory Commission is a rare case indeed. Beginning life as an agency (the Atomic Energy Commission) charged with the task of promoting the use of nuclear energy, a quarter century later it was asked to turn 180 degrees and regulate the very industry it had helped to establish. How does it cope with such a major shift in organizational mission? Do its decisions reflect this major reorientation? Can long-term relationships between the NRC and its former client (public utilities) be ignored? Is guarding the "public interest" a more slippery mission than promoting nuclear energy? These questions are at the crux of this research.

The Development of Bureaucracy

Weber links the development of bureaucracy with modern mass democracy. However, there are two basic principles of democracy that are at odds with bureaucratic theory. First, democracy seeks to prevent the development of a closed-status group of officials in the interest of a universal accessibility to public office. The bureaucracy, on the other hand, provides that only experts can hold positions. Second, democracy seeks to minimize the authority of officialdom in the interest of expanding the "sphere of public opinion as far as practicable."[4] One way of doing this is to require regular and frequent elections of officials. By contrast, bureaucratic theory calls for bureaucrats to retain their positions indefinitely.

Sources of Bureaucratic Power

Over time, the bureaucracy may come to occupy a position of considerable power within its jurisdictional sphere. The bureaucracy's power derives from three major sources. The first of these is the expertise of the bureaucrat. In the case of the public bureaucracy, the legislature or some other body of elected officials is—nominally at least—the master of the bureaucracy. Yet the master rarely has the degree of technical expertise that the servant, bureaucracy, possesses. In practice, this means that the political master plays the role of dilettante to the bureaucracy's expert. Particularly in

---

4   Ibid., p. 226.

the case of highly technical fields, the master often must defer to the more knowledgeable servant.

The second source of the bureaucracy's power is the professionalism of bureaucrats and their ability to guard their knowledge from outsiders. Each profession has a body of knowledge that is uniquely its own. In order to become a member of the profession, the aspiring candidate must go through a well-defined right of passage that ordinarily culminates in some sort of certification process. For example, if a person wishes to become a lawyer, he or she attends an accredited law school, graduates, takes the bar examination, and—provided he or she passes the exam—is admitted into the practice of law.

The bureaucracy that can closely guard its body of knowledge improves its staying power. Technical professions are often very successful because they have learned to guard carefully a relatively small but highly complex body of knowledge that is theirs. In many states, beauticians and cosmetologists are just such a group. With the cooperation of legislative bodies, they have developed certification procedures that very effectively limit entry into their ranks to people who have successfully maneuvered through their certification process. While limiting entry into the field, certification also helps to preserve the technical credibility of the group within its field of expertise.

On the other hand, professionals who fail to establish a certification process that is generally accepted by practitioners of the profession and those who hire them leave open the door for outsiders to encroach on their turf. The planning profession is a good example of this phenomenon. Planners are represented by two separate but related groups: the American Planning Association and the American Institute of Certified Planners. The latter has a testing and certification procedure. In spite of the existence of certification for planners, one need not be certified to seek, win, or hold most jobs in planning. In this sense, the profession has failed as a profession to carve a niche for itself.

Language plays an important role in establishing and protecting professional turf. Each profession has its own technical language (or jargon), literature, and lore, mastery of which is an important component of any certification process. The more technical—or less commonly understandable— the language, the easier it is for the profession to establish its expertise and maintain its exclusivity.

The third source of the bureaucracy's power lies in its relationship with its clientele group. Each bureaucracy that comes into being and flourishes does so because it can identify and colonize a specific group of people who can reap the benefits of the activities of the bureaucracy. The more powerful the clientele group, the more tenacious the bureaucracy.

Without a clientele group, the bureaucracy ceases to exist. As an example, we can point to the March of Dimes, whose original goal was to help stamp out polio. With its help (primarily financial), two polio vaccines were developed, the once dreaded disease was all but eradicated, and the March of Dimes lost its clientele. There is a happy ending, however, as the organization adopted a new clientele group, that embracing research into all birth defects. This particular story has become part of organizational lore.

The relationship between the bureaucracy and its clientele group is one of mutual dependency. The clientele group benefits from the expertise of the bureaucracy employed in its behalf; the bureaucracy depends on its continuing sound relationship with its clientele for its very existence. Weber believed that the interdependency between the bureaucracy and its clientele group is of major importance in the establishment and growth of the bureaucratic form.

Weber recognized the staying power of the bureaucracy. "Once it is fully established," he said, "bureaucracy is among those social structures which is hardest to destroy. Bureaucracy is the means of carrying 'community action' over into a rationally ordered 'societal action.'"[5] Weber's view of the bureaucracy has a dialectical element to it. On the one hand, he found fault with the tendency of bureaucracy to elevate bureaucrats, by virtue of their superior and specialized knowledge, to the status of a mandarin caste. On the other hand, he saw in the bureaucracy a means of limiting the potential for self-interested actions by elected officials (especially corrupt officials). Bureaucrats, subject to the judgment of their peers and the need to maintain the support of their clientele, can be held accountable for their actions.[6]

Weber discussed the inherent differences between the bureaucratic organization and charismatic structure in great detail, acknowledging that both of these structures are characterized by a "most important peculiarity": "permanence. As a permanent structure with a system of rational rules, bureaucracy is fashioned to meet calculable and recurrent needs by means of a normal routine. The provisioning of all demands that go beyond those of everyday routine has had, in principle, an entirely heterogeneous, namely, a charismatic foundation."[7]

In all other characteristics, bureaucracy and charismatic structures are mirror images. Whereas bureaucracy depends on a routinized organization of offices, charismatic structures have no such system, no idea of a career, promotions, or salaries. "Charisma knows only inner determination and

---

5   Ibid., p. 228.
6   Ibid., p. 18.
7   Ibid., p. 245.

inner restraint."[8] Charismatic leaders can maintain their following only as long as their are recognized by those people (that clientele group) to whom they believe they have been sent.

"The sharp contrast," says Weber, "between charisma and a 'patri-archal' structure that rests upon the ordered base of the 'household' lies in (the) rejection of rational economic conduct."[9] Charismatic leaders are specifically uninterested in the economic gains to be had in this world. They are instead concerned with the success of their missions.

Weber characterizes charisma as a disappearing artifact of an earlier time: "It is the fate of charisma, wherever it comes into the permanent institutions of a community, to give way to powers of tradition or of ra-tional socialization. This waning of charisma generally indicates the dimin-ishing importance of individual action. And of all those powers that lessen the importance of individual action, the most irresistible is rational dis-cipline."[10]

Weber contends that aside from eradicating personal charisma, disci-pline also eradicates stratification on the basis of status groups. The result-ing destratification promotes the impersonality in the application of dis-cipline, similar to the more general notion of bureaucratic impersonality. "Unfailingly neutral, it places itself at the disposal of every power that claims its service and knows how to promote it."[11] Weber admits that this does not prevent bureaucracy from being intrinsically alien and opposed to charisma. Indeed, this admission suggests that groups who would claim the services of a specific bureaucracy must gain knowledge if they hope to influence the bureaucracy. Such groups must first learn about the larger system in which the bureaucracy operates and identify the target bureaucracy. They must then learn the machinations of the bureaucracy in order to increase their influence.

In Weber's view, discipline grows along with modern emphasis on the rationalization of the supply of economic and political demands. As the phenomenon comes into being, it brings with it a restriction in the impor-tance of charisma and of individually differentiated conduct. As this process continues, charisma is retained as an anomaly, coming into play during short-lived outpourings of mass emotion, such as might be observed in an election. Such outpourings thus legitimate a charismatic leader, resulting in "routinized charisma."[12]

---

[8] Ibid., p. 246.
[9] Ibid., p. 247.
[10] Ibid., p. 253.
[11] Ibid., p. 254.
[12] Ibid., p. 262.

Weber discusses routinized charisma specifically as it relates to sovereign rulers, whose only real power is their power to influence. It is not far-fetched, however, to apply the concept of routinized charisma to the general class of elected officials in the United States insofar as they do not implement policy, but leave that to bureaucrats.[13]

Weber, then, develops a world wherein all that can be routinized is routinized. All power structures, be they bureaucratic or charismatic, need legitimacy in order to continue. Decisions are made in a rational fashion, that rationality being formal in nature.

In terms of Weber's ideas about economically rational action, we begin with a bureaucracy, staffed by bureaucrats who wish to maintain their jobs and, if possible, to earn promotions. The bureaucrats must do their jobs well in order to find an optimal arrangement whereby they can satisfy the competing pressures of both their peers and the members of the bureaucracy's clientele group. Hence, the bureaucrat and the bureaucracy depend— at least in part—for their continuing health and viability on their ability to satisfy their clients. Thus, we must include the needs and desires of clients (sometimes expressed in a highly vocal manner) in any Weberian model of bureaucratic decision-making.

The Organization-Client Relationship

Literature from public administration theory reiterates time and again the importance of the relationship between the organization and its clients. Conventional thought hypothesizes a three-party system in the decision-making process: organization, legislature, and clients. Simon's model includes three parties as well, although it is drawn to include entrepreneurs, employees and customers.[14] In Simon's model, the legislature is analogous to customers and, as such, the public organization is bound to respond to the will of elected officials. Simon's argument in favor of the legislature as the public agency's customer centers on the legislature's role as keeper of the purse from which the organization is funded.

This concept is in conflict with Weberian principles and, in later work with March, Simon adopts the more conventional approach to clients, that is, defining clients as the term has previously been used in this paper, and acknowledges the importance of clients in the decision-making process.[15] In another article, Simon (along with Smithburg and Thompson) admits that while the legislature provides both legal authority and funds for

---

[13] Ibid., p. 264.

[14] Herbert A. Simon, *Administrative Behavior* (New York: Free Press, 1945), p. 18.

[15] James G. March, and *Organizations* (New York: John Wiley and Sons, 1958), p. 39.

the organization, the public—clients—give the legislature its political support (and hence its legitimacy) and thus are integral in the process.[16]

Moreover, Long reiterates this idea when he says that "bureaucracy is recognized by all interested groups as a major channel of representation to such an extent that Congress rightly feels the competition of a rival."[17] In fact, Wilson argues that the original purpose of creating client-oriented organizations is not to subsidize or to regulate, but r. ther to promote the needs and the will of the client.[18]

Especially in its early stages, the organization benefits greatly from the support of its clientele, according to Holden.[19] He adds that agencies are formed, and new responsibilities assumed by the agency, because of a perceived need for reform, improvement, or development in the agency's substantive field—and on behalf of its clients. In its early stages, the agency must consolidate its power. Power, says Holden, "is organized around constituency."[20] Clients are important.

The link between clients and agency power is important. Rourke makes the point that the greater the number of the agency's clients, the more powerful the agency. He notes further that a greater geographical dispersion of clientele likewise enhances an agency's power. Rourke notes that there are other clientele characteristics that can strengthen the agency, namely, cohesion and commitment: "However large it may be, a clientele that is weak in certain other salient respects will not be in a position to give effective political assistance. A small clientele that is highly self-conscious and dedicated to the pursuit of certain tangible objectives that it shares with the agency can in the last analysis be much more helpful than a large clientele that has neither of these characteristics."[21]

Moreover, Rourke maintains that in general an agency will prefer to draw its support from a variety of groups rather than from a single one. In so doing, the agency has a power base that is broad, yet diffuse enough that none of the groups can gain substantial control over the agency.[22]

---

[16] Herbert A. Simon; Donald W. Smithburg, and Victor A. Thompson, "The Struggle for Organizational Survival," in *Bureaucratic Power in National Politics,* by Francis E. Rourke (Boston: Little, Brown and Co., 1978), p. 18.

[17] Norton E. Long, "Power and Administration," in Rourke, *Bureaucratic Power in National Politics,* p. 11.

[18] James Q. Wilson, "The Rise of the Bureaucratic State," in Rourke, *Bureaucratic Power in National Politics,* p. 64.

[19] Matthew Holden, Jr., "Imperialism in Bureaucracy," in Rourke, *Bureaucratic Power in National Politics,* p. 168.

[20] Ibid.

[21] Francis E. Rourke, "Variations in Agency Power," in Rourke, *Bureaucratic Power in National Politics,* p. 230.

[22] Ibid., p. 232.

Acknowledging the link between clients and agency power, Schick asks, why not give an agency to the politically deprived? In response to his own question, he says, "A weak clientele breeds a weak agency, a condition that is common to anti-poverty agencies and correctional institutions."[23]

Inasmuch as clients contribute greatly to the agency's power, the goals of the organization and those of the client are intertwined. According to Simon, "the objectives of the customer are rather directly related to the objectives of the organizations."[24] Furthermore, Gibson maintains, organizational goals are largely set and modified as a result of the relationship between the organization and its environment, clients being an integral part of that environment.[25]

Clients are important in determining organizational goals, according to Thompson. The relationship between the organization and its environment is one of exchange. Unless the organization is offering something desirable—in the estimation of its clientele—the organization will be lacking an element essential to its survival. Thompson points out that informal goals, in addition to the formal statement of goals found in charters, articles of incorporation, or institutional advertising, are worthy of inspection and consideration.[26]

The unity of purpose that the organization and its clientele share is not without its dilemma. Finer asks this question: does the organization work on behalf of what its clientele needs or does it do what its clients want?[27] Finer argues that the agency that seeks to prosper will try to satisfy the wants of its clientele rather than its needs. He further notes that organizations react specifically to the expressed desires of their clients.[28] As Friedrich says on this subject, "The customer is always right."[29]

So important are clients to organizations that Fesler notes that one version of democratic, participative decision-making expresses the ideal of

---

[23] Allen Schick, "The Trauma of Politics: Public Administration in the Sixties," in *American Public Administration: Past, Present, and Future,* edited by Frederick C. Mosher (University: University of Alabama Press, 1976), p. 155.

[24] Simon, *Administrative Behaviour,* p. 18.

[25] Frank Gibson, "Organizations and Their Environments: The School System as a Focus," in *Public Administration: Readings in Institutions, Processes, Behavior, Policy,* edited by R.T. Golembiewski, F. Gibson, and G.Y. Cornog (Chicago: Rand McNally College Publishing Co., 1976), p. 257.

[26] James D. Thompson, *Organizations in Action* (New York: McGraw-Hill Book Co., 1967), pp. 28-29.

[27] Herman Finer, "Administrative Responsibility in Democratic Government," in Rourke, *Bureaucratic Power in National Politics,* p. 412.

[28] Ibid.

[29] Carl J. Friedrich, "Public Policy and the Nature of Administrative Responsibility," in Rourke, *Bureaucratic Power in National Politics,* p. 408.

proactive policymaking for and control of the agency by its clientele.[30] This model relies heavily upon client participation in the decision-making process.

Grodzins suggests that federal and state programs could not exist without the lobbying efforts of client groups.[31] Likewise, Harmon emphasizes the importance of client groups in decision-making. While allowing that elections provide clients with a formal and regular venue for influencing the legislature in their own behalf, he argues that the voting process is incapable of coping with the day-to-day demands of clients, who are better served by a continuing, longer-term relationship with the agency.[32]

A serious dilemma arises in the relationships between client groups and their organizations, in spite of all the preceding evidence to recommend the union. As described earlier, an important tenet of Weberian bureaucracy is that equal treatment of individuals is the rule. There is a good reason for this rule, according to Downs: if rules governing decisions concerning clients are such that reasonably consistent responses result, then the agency can avoid charges of discrimination or favoritism.[33] In Thompson's estimation, former U.S. President Gerald Ford's pardon of Richard Nixon was an act of favoritism, and the public outcry against the pardon is an example of why such favoritism (or "compassionate behavior," as he calls it) is undesirable as a standard operating procedure for an organization.[34]

But when equal treatment is carried to an extreme, March and Simon describe it as "rigidity of behavior," another undesirable modus operandi for an organization. According to these authors, "the rigidity of behavior increases the amount of difficulty with clients of the organization and complicates the achievement of client satisfaction—a near universal goal."[35]

The organization, then, must exercise balance in its dealings with its clientele if it wishes to maintain its viability.

There is ample evidence to indicate the importance of clients in the organizational decision-making process. While this is interesting in the abstract, it tells us little or nothing in and of itself. The literature on organi-

[30] James N. Fesler, "Public Administration and the Social Sciences: 1946-1960," in Mosher, *American Public Administration*, p. 119.
[31] Morton Grodzins, "The Many American Governments and Outdoor Recreation," in Golembiewski et al., *Public Administration*, p. 343.
[32] Michael M. Harmon, "Administrative Policy Formulations," in Golembiewski et al., *Public Administration*, p. 345.
[33] Anthony Downs, *Inside Bureaucracy* (Boston: Little, Brown and Co., 1966), pp. 70-71.
[34] Victor A. Thompson, *Bureaucracy and the Modern World* (Morristown N.J.: General Learning Press, 1976), p. 124.
[35] March and Simon, *Organizations*, p. 39.

zations and clients suggests specific directions in research on the nature of their relationship. If we agree with Long that the original purpose of creating client-oriented organizations is to promote the needs and will of the clients, then we must necessarily be concerned with discovering the goals of both the organization and its clients.[36] Likewise, Rourke's discussion of variations in agency power as a function of the nature of its clientele points to a need to explore the nature of the clients involved in the Bailly case.[37] Thompson's warning that formal statements of purpose are not sufficient to tell us all we know about organizations and clients suggests that a foray into informal structures is well advised.[38]

The organization's interest in serving its client group has its foundation in rationality and rational action. Specifically, the organization seeks to ensure its continuing existence by serving its client. The literature on rationality is broad, and is considered only where directly related to this research. However, both Weber and Habermas have written on rationality and their discussions are considered below.

Weber, Habermas, and Rationality

Rationality was, for Weber, a topic of considerable interest. Weber's work on rationality suggests an implicit but intense tug-of-war between individual and societal orientations in his own mind. One indication of this struggle is Weber's reluctance to provide a single, all-purpose definition of rationality. "A thing is never irrational in itself, but only from a particular . . . point of view. For the unbeliever, every religious way of life is irrational, for the hedonist, every ascetic standard."[39]

Brubaker, critiquing Weber, writes, "This passage expresses with consummate simplicity two axioms of Weber's social thought. First, rationality does not inhere in things, but is ascribed to them. Secondly, rationality is a relational concept: a thing can be rational (or irrational) only from a particular point of view, never in and of itself."[40]

Weber distinguishes between means-rational and ends-rational actions. By means-rational action, or "formal rationality," Weber refers to the strategy an individual follows to achieve his or her goal.[41] As will become

---

[36] Long, "Power and Administration," p. 11.

[37] Rourke, "Variations in Agency Power," p. 230.

[38] Thompson, *Organizations in Action*, p. 28-29.

[39] Max Weber, *The Protestant Ethic and the Spirit of Capitalism*, trans. Talcott Parsons (New York: Scribner's, 1958), p. 194, n. 9; quoted in Rogers Brubaker, *The Limits of Rationality* (Boston: George Allen and Unwin, 1984), p. 35.

[40] Brubaker, *Limits of Rationality*, p. 35.

[41] Max Weber, *Economy and Society*, ed. Guenther Roth and Claus Wittich. (Berkeley: University of California Press, 1968, pp. 85-86.

evident, the NRC adopted a means-rational approach to its decisions on the Bailly nuclear facility. By ends-rational action, or "substantive rationality," Weber refers to the goal choices of individuals, closely intertwined with individually held values.[42] Actions hold intrinsic value for the actor, regardless of the outcome, and are ends in and of themselves. For this reason, there can be no objective measure of ends-rational action. As Brubaker puts it, "Formal rationality is a matter of fact, substantive rationality a matter of value."[43]

Habermas's Theory of Communicative Action

Jurgen Habermas presents an alternative view of rationality that is closely related to his theory of communicative action. Habermas's "concept of communicative action presupposes language as the medium for a kind of reaching understanding, in the course of which participants, through relating to a world, reciprocally raise validity claims that can be accepted or contested."[44]

The participants use argumentation to build support for their particular positions and reach an understanding. The strategy for achieving understanding is to develop a rational argument.

Language serves to provide a framework within which human interaction becomes meaningful. Because people share language, they may engage in argumentation designed to achieve understanding. According to the theory of communicative action, there is an objective reality, and in debates about this objective reality, the more rational argument—that which raises greater validity claims—should hold sway.

Habermas stresses the importance of the development of a framework of social norms among the communicating parties. His concept of communicative action presumes an objective reality about which meaningful argumentation can occur, permitting the participants to reach an understanding. Weber's concept of substantive rationality is directly at odds with Habermas's concept of rationality as defined by his theory of communicative action. First, Habermas's theory assumes that reaching understanding is an important goal of human interaction. Weber, on the other hand, recognizes that "rational exchange is only possible when both parties expect to profit from it or when one is under compulsion because of his own need or the other's economic power."[45]

---

[42] Ibid.

[43] Brubaker, p. 36.

[44] Jurgen Habermas, *The Theory of Communicative Action*, Vol. 1, *Reason and the Rationalization of Society*, trans. Thomas McCarthy (Boston: Beacon Press, 1981), p. 99.

[45] Weber, *Economy and Society*, p. 73.

More important, however, validity claims that have values at their core represent a source of irreconcilable conflict for Weber. No amount of rational appeal is guaranteed to sway an individual from his values. Argumentation based on values—substantive rationality—is often futile. In Weber's view, "'Scientific' pleading is meaningless in principle because the various value spheres of the world stand in irreconcilable conflict with each other."[46]

Habermas's theory of communicative action also takes account of the problem of divergent issue definition: "A definition of the situation by another party that prima facie diverges from one's own presents a problem of a peculiar sort; for in cooperative processes of interpretation no participant has a monopoly on correct interpretation. For both parties the interpretive task consists in incorporating the other's interpretation of the situation into one's own in such a way that in the revised version 'his' external world and 'my' external world can—against the background of 'our' lifeworld—be relativized in relation to 'the' world, and the divergent situation definitions can be brought to coincide sufficiently."[47] Rational communicative action would be the means to accomplish this task.

The Weberian concept suggests that an appeal on rational grounds would be ineffectual in the instance described above. "Not ideas, but material and ideal interests, directly govern men's conduct."[48]

Whereas Habermas does not discuss the role of clients, he emphasizes the importance of communication in the decision-making process. Habermas's theory of communicative action has been used by a pair of geographers, Roweis and Forester, to form the basis of their tightly constrained and reactive theories of planning. This is in contrast with a planning theory underpinned by Weberian theory, which is much more dynamic and proactive.

For example, according to Roweis and Forester, Habermas's theory of communicative action suggests that the major role of the public servant is as a mediator among groups in disagreement. Such a theory immediately fails to recognize that certain public agencies—namely, regulatory agencies—are vested with adjudicative authority and the authority to promulgate rules as well. They serve as arbitrators rather than as mediators. In Weberian theory, the organization would be expected to consider the needs or wishes of its clientele as it makes decisions that affect its clients. In the Habermas approach, the organization relies primarily on its ability to define, direct, and if necessary, limit communication to enable participants

---

[46] Gerth and Mills, *From Max Weber*, p. 147.
[47] Habermas, *Theory of Communicative Action*, p. 100.
[48] Gerth and Mills, *From Max Weber*, p. 280.

in the conflict to achieve an understanding. By thus controlling communication, the organization promotes and, if successful, assures, continued existence.

In a 1981 article, Roweis takes a Marxian perspective as he claims that planning is a tool of the state, which is, in turn, heavily influenced by capital.[49] He goes on to explain that the state has developed apparatuses that rely on "pre-politics processing of information."[50] These apparatuses are designed to ascertain the will of the masses and to use that information to forestall a revolution. When, in a later article, Roweis argues that urban planning is the professional mediation of territorial politics, it comes as no surprise.[51] Forester echoes this view by claiming that planning practice may be understood as a structure of communicative action.[52]

While it is clear that communication plays a significant role in planning, the interpretation of the theory of communicative action that Roweis and Forester adopt cannot adequately deal with planning agencies that operate in a regulatory mode, such as the Nuclear Regulatory Commission. Such agencies are vested with authority that goes beyond the limits of mediation and persuasive strategies. Regulatory agencies have the power to adjudicate, arbitrate, and even to promulgate.

Mediation may be the first-line strategy, even for a regulatory agency, but adjudication remains as its final word. Whether we regard planning agencies as mediators or as adjudicators has important implications for our view of planners. The Habermas-derived approach (mediator) minimizes the relationship between the organization and its clients. The Weberian approach (adjudicative) implies a close and critical linkage between the organization and its clients. Moreover, the Weberian approach recognizes that the organization has some flexibility in the way it carries out its responsibilities. While some organizations adjudicate, others actively promote the needs of their clients within a larger public policy sphere.

The Habermas communicative action approach ignores clients and has planners using their expertise to enlighten competing groups in order to help resolve their differences. The planners may use their expertise to control the outcome of a situation by controlling the communication on the issue. The Weberian approach, on the other hand, would have the planners

[49] Shoukry Roweis, "Urban Planning in Early and Late Capitalist Society: Outline of a Theoretical Perspective," in *Urbanization and Urban Planning in a Capitalist Society*, ed. Dear and Scott (New York: Methuen, 1981).

[50] Ibid.

[51] S. Roweis, "Urban Planning as Professional Mediation of Territorial Politics," *Environment and Planning D: Society and Space*, 1982, n. 1, pp. 139-62.

[52] J. Forester, "The Geography of Planning Practice," *Environment and Planning D: Society and Space*, 1983, no. 1, pp. 163-80.

use their expertise to determine the best alternative to promote the goals of its clients. This approach assumes a proactive agency, rather than a reactive agency.

The Habermas approach implies that planners need to be expert in controlling communication as a means of achieving resolution. The Weberian approach implies that planners must exercise their expertise in their substantive fields. Indeed, the Weberian model speaks to the need for planners to develop their expertise and use it as a tool to promote their just organizational goals.

Just as Habermas's theory of communicative action is valuable as a counterpoint to reiterate the importance of clients in the decision-making process, so is Roweis and Forester's use of this theory valuable as a means to understand the special relationship between the planning agency and its clientele. The Bailly case study relies on a Weberian interpretation of the relationship between the organization and its clients. The previous discussion, then, helps to clarify that relationship.

The Technocratic Model

Interestingly, Habermas discusses a technocratic model of organizations wherein politicians become "the mere agent of a scientific intelligentsia which, in concrete circumstances, elaborates the objective implications and requirements of available techniques and resources as well as of optimal strategies and rules of control."[53] Because of the overwhelming expertise of scientists, the ability of politicians to make decisions is illusory at best. Experts, advantaged by their superior knowledge, are in a position to limit—either by explicit design or by accidental omission—the knowledge they pass on to policymakers. The politician is further isolated from the decision-making process if the expert is also cast as an advisor.

This technocratic model includes clients, but they serve as legitimators of politicians in the electoral process. Given Habermas's earlier assertion that politicians' actual decision-making power is limited by the knowledge of experts within the organization, this role as legitimator is insignificant in the decision-making process as a whole.

And yet Habermas hints that there is potential for expanding the role of clients, which he characterizes as a "politically functioning public." That potential for expansion continues to hinge on the political connection, especially the connection through public opinion: "If politicians were strictly subjected to objective necessity, a politically functioning public could at best legitimate the administrative personnel and judge the professional qualifi-

---

53 Jurgen Habermas, *Toward a Rational Society, Student Protest, Science, and Politics,* trans. Jeremy J. Shapiro (Boston: Beacon Press, 1970), p. 63.

cations of salaried officials. But if the latter were of comparable qualifications it would in principle be a matter of indifference which competing elite group obtained power."[54]

Weber's model explicitly acknowledges that the public has a point of entry into the decision-making process at a point other than the electoral process. To reiterate, Weber emphasizes that whoever can learn to use the bureaucracy can make it work for them. And they need not be a member of an elite class: an obvious example of a nonelite who has made the bureaucracy work for her is the so-called welfare queen, who knows the welfare system inside and out, and as a consequence of her knowledge, is able to maximize her benefits.

The interdependency relationship between the organization and the client of Weber's model conflicts with another assertion of Habermas, namely, that "the articulation of needs in accordance with technical knowledge can be ratified exclusively in the consciousness of the political actors themselves."[55] On the contrary, given the multiplicity of points of entry for clients in organizations, the articulation of needs that Habermas mentions can be ratified within the parameters of the organization-client relationship. Additionally, in some circumstances, clients bring with them their own technical knowledge. This technical knowledge becomes especially evident in the setting of public hearings. In this setting, wherein a forum for public input is guaranteed, it is common to observe many well-informed—if not actually expert—private citizens.

Habermas is astutely interested in how the rationalization process influences modern society.[56] However, his interest in organizational structures is incidental to his overriding interest in the rationalization process. Organizations for Weber, on the other hand, constitute a fundamental concern. Weber is interested in organizations as a consequence of a changing society, and he seems equally interested in the consequences of organizational structure and actions.

Habermas's concern with rationality in communication has led him to attempt to systematize Weber, "to reconstruct his project as a whole."[57] This desire of Habermas could be perceived as a desire to impose order where order does not necessarily exist in reality. Weber's leaving "his work behind in a fragmentary state"[58] (as Habermas puts it) may be a reflection of ideological differences between the two men. Indeed, Habermas's approach implies a view of the world that emphasizes society rather than the

---

54 Ibid., p. 68.
55 Ibid., p. 75.
56 Habermas, *Theory of Communicative Action*, p. 155.
57 Ibid., p. 143.
58 Ibid.

individual. In contrast, Weber is concerned with what happens to the individual as society becomes more rationalized, i.e., bureaucratized. One manifestation of this is Weber's unwillingness to define tightly what he means by rationality. His distinction between formal and substantive rationality seems to reflect a desire to understand how the individual fits into the larger society. More important, it implies a desire to retain the individual as a focal point of study.

Both Habermas and Weber criticize capitalism. Weber's criticisms, however, emphasize the threat to the individual personality created by the increasing rationality of the state, as epitomized by its administrative system (i.e., the bureaucracy). The neo-Marxist framework, as developed by Roweis and Forester in their treatment of Habermas, emphasizes control of individuals by the state and capitalist institutions as opposed to a more generalized concern with loss of individual freedom and personality. In the extreme, the Weberian would expect little difference between a Marxist and a capitalist state. The state, by its very nature, seeks to achieve and maintain control of its citizenry to achieve its goals, regardless of the economic system it adopts. The state is formally rational in this respect. The Weberian view is more concerned with the nature and the extent of state control and the effects of that control on the individual.

The relationship between the organization and its clientele is one of great importance. Although there is a well-developed body of research on this topic, it is clear that there is much more to learn.

Clients and Regulatory Organizations

The preceding literature review covered several distinct themes: bureaucracies, clients and organizations, and rationality. This section brings together these diverse themes in an effort to develop a coherent theory of regulatory organizations and their clients.

The study of organizations has continued over several decades. In general, studies of this sort treat the organization as a unitary actor. According to March and Olsen, this is but a single symptom of a more serious problem with the literature (and research) on organizations. The approach to organizations has emphasized the institution as an arena "within which political behavior, driven by more fundamental factors, occurs. From a normative point of view, ideas that embedded morality in institutions, such as law and bureaucracy, and that emphasized citizenship as a foundation for personal identity, have given way to ideas of moral individualism and an emphasis on conflicting interests."[59]

---

[59] J.G. March and J.P. Olsen, "The New Institutionalism: Organizational Factors in Political Life," *American Political Science Review*, v. 78, (1984): 734.

Moreover, the authors contend, there has been a pervasive view among social scientists that the development of theory is progressive, along with an acceptance of the idea that there is a "more or less inexorable historical movement toward some more 'advanced' level."[60] This view often results in theory deduced from historical events.

The idea of an "inexorable march toward the truth"[61] is also prevalent in the natural sciences. In recent years, Stephen Jay Gould has challenged this phenomenon in the natural sciences in much the same way March and Olsen have challenged it in the social sciences. Gould rejects "an approach to the history of science that rapes the past for seeds and harbingers of later views; such a perspective only makes sense within the abandoned faith that science progresses by accumulation toward absolute truth."[62]

Modern research on organizations, according to March and Olsen, is less sure of itself than in Weber's day. New complexities enter the picture. Organizations interact with their environments in a variety of ways and they face greater ambiguity and uncertainty, as evidenced by a proliferation of literature on organizational environments. Empirical evidence is not so easily synthesized and analyzed as in earlier times. March and Olsen call for clearer direction in organizational theory.

The number and variety of organizations increases annually. Whereas once organizations could be tidily labeled as either public or private, variations and admixtures of these two types now clutter the organizational landscape. Not-for-profit organizations fall into neither category (or maybe into both). And in some instances private firms are assuming functions that had previously been exclusively limited to the public sector; prison administration is the best example. Public-private cooperative ventures are yet another variation on the same theme.

Even within the public sector, things have changed. The traditional separation of powers (executive, legislative, and judicial) has become blurred. The regulatory agency, a prime example, exercises all three powers simultaneously. (The legal framework of the regulatory agency is discussed at greater length in the next chapter.)

Coincidentally, the "new institutionalism," as March and Olsen call the increasing complexity of organizational analysis, has arisen within the same time frame as the rise of the regulatory agency.[63]

---

[60] Ibid., p. 737.

[61] S.J. Gould, *The Mismeasure of Man* (New York: W.W. Norton and Co., 1981), p. 23.

[62] S.J. Gould, *Ontogeny and Phylogeny* (Cambridge, Mass.: The Belknap Press of Harvard University Press, 1977), p. 16.

[63] R.B. Stewart, "Reconstitutive Law," presented as the Simon E. Sobeloff lecture at the University of Maryland Law School in April 1985.

I am here suggesting that the development of the regulatory agency is of great significance. The regulatory agency is not an individual organizational mutant, but forms the basis for an entirely new organizational species. By virtue of its three powers, the regulatory agency is inherently more interactive than its progenitors. The regulatory agency has authority to promulgate rules, implement them, and adjudicate on issues within its functional jurisdiction. It is particularly within its adjudicatory authority that the regulatory agency best exhibits its interactive nature, providing an outlet for "moral individualism and an emphasis on conflicting interests."[64]

In light of the rise of the regulatory agency, is it any wonder that current organization theory is in a state of flux? Is it any wonder that the new institutionalism emphasizes the relative autonomy of institutions? Or that it treats political phenomena as the aggregate consequences of individual behavior?

Indeed, not only has the evolution of the regulatory agency changed the basic order of organizations, the regulatory agency is itself in a state of flux. The organizational species "regulator" is not sterile and has produced descendants.

The Nuclear Regulatory Commission is a good example. The NRC is, in its functional area, a first-generation regulator. Beginning as a promoter (the AEC), the agency mutated into a regulator. The staying power of organizations and the reproduction of institutions are almost truisms. But what of the nature of the reproduction of institutions? Is the second generation a clone of the first? Does the regulator specifically mutate in some way in response to its environment?

In moving toward an extension of organization theory, I am struck by both the interactive nature and the relative autonomy of the regulatory agency. The regulator is exposed at several points of entry to potential clients within its functional jurisdiction. Its adjudicatory authority assures that it will hear at least two sides of every issue before it. That same authority, in fact, attracts clients, along with their adversaries, to the regulatory organization. The power of the regulator to promulgate rules further assures that it will attract potential clients and adversaries alike who may seek to influence rule-making. Finally, the implementation of rules is another point of entry in the regulatory agency for potential clients and adversaries.

The attraction of the regulator for both client and adversary alike is an important concept. The extension of access by adversaries to regulatory agencies is a development that has occurred over the past twenty years in the United States. "This development was in substantial part a judicial and legislative response to the previously noted fears that informal accommo-

---

[64] March and Olsen, "The New Institutionalism," p. 734.

dation between regulators and regulated reflected backdoor industry 'capture.'"[65] Along with this development has come an implicit assumption that the regulator should act in what is commonly called the public interest, an assumption that often bears an uncanny resemblance to the position adopted by adversaries of the regulated industry. Indeed, the question of who is the true client of the regulator may arise.

Over time, the resulting interaction between the regulator and its potential clients begins to leave its imprint on the regulatory agency. Little by little, the regulator responds to the complex interaction of which it is the focus.

And make no mistake, the interaction is extremely complex. In the first instance, the regulatory agency is a product of legislation. As such, its very genes, if you will, bear the imprint of its progenitors. Some, like Lowi, would argue that the regulator is the result of a legislative version of gene splicing, producing an agency that is designed to render specific outcomes, perhaps even to favor a predetermined client.[66]

Once the regulator goes out into the world, however, because it has the power to promulgate rules within its functional jurisdiction, it can reproduce itself without further assistance from the legislature. Occasionally, there may be exchanges between the legislative and regulatory "gene pools." This occurs under two circumstances: (1) when the regulator mutates excessively from its original legislative design (the reorganization of the AEC is an example); or (2) when the regulator is under extreme pressure from the potential clients in its organizational environment (the NRC's effort to gain legislative approval to license nuclear plants in the absence of state emergency evacuation plans, for example).

One component of the regulator's organizational environment is the judicial branch of government. The regulator is subject to judicial review. This control, however, is relatively weak, particularly where the regulator is responsible for a highly technical area, as in the case of the NRC. This point is discussed more fully in a later chapter.

Clients and Potential Clients

The regulator's environment also contains other sources of influence in the form of clients, both actual and potential. The question of who is the client of the regulator is relevant in the development of a theory of regulatory organizations. In determining the client of the regulator, there are two competing but equally plausible approaches.

---

[65] R.B. Stewart, "The Discontents of Legalism: Interest Group Relations in Administrative Regulation," *Wisconsin Law Review*, n. 3 (1985): 666.

[66] T.J. Lowi, *The End of Liberalism* (New York: W.W. Norton and Co., 1969).

One approach is to argue that the regulator should represent the public interest against the interests of the regulated industry; the second emphasizes the rule of capture. The regulator, because if its broad grant of power, is in a position to promote the interests of either the regulated industry or the public interest. Therefore, we may speak of clients and adversaries, or we may reconceptualize this dynamic as clients and potential clients.

In general, as Rourke notes, an organization prefers a large, loosely organized client group as opposed to a small group. Such a client, it is thought, provides a broad base of support for the organization without exercising tight control. However, size alone does not assure that a client group will succeed in its efforts to capture a specific target organization.[67] Because of its broad grant of powers, the regulator need not be overly concerned with tight control from its client. Indeed, it may logically seek to win the support of a "small clientele that is highly self-conscious and dedicated to the pursuit of certain tangible objectives that it shares with the agency."[68] Hence, the historical capture of regulators by the regulated industry.

From time to time, however, the regulator takes a position against the regulated industry, in support of the public interest (normally the potential client). The question then arises, under what circumstances will a regulator be likely to support its potential client against its historical client? As a general rule, overwhelming public opinion, manifested in a variety of ways, seems to induce the regulator to support its potential client. It is possible, in fact, that it is only at these times that the regulator has adequate guidance from its potential client, the public interest, to act on its behalf.

Public opinion may be transmitted to the regulator by collective action, taking the form of demonstrations or other visible forms of action. Or, the transmittal may be more indirect, as potential clients bombard their legislators with letters requesting greater control of the regulator. Often, collective action is precipitated by historical events. In the nuclear industry, the energy shocks created by the Arab oil embargo, and the accidents at Three Mile Island and Chernobyl, are examples of historical events that triggered collective action. Often these three factors (collective action, legislative pressure, and historical events) seem to occur simultaneously, making it impossible to determine to which (or to which combination) of these the regulator responds. The exact determination of the causal links is not within the purview of this research.

What is important here, however, is that the regulator does respond to its clients, be they actual or potential, and that the regulator may choose which client to favor, regardless of its organizational mission. Indeed, the

---

[67] Rourke, "Variations in Agency Power," p. 230.
[68] Ibid.

regulator, like the human species, seeks to reproduce itself, and may choose its client on the basis of its desire for survival as an organizational species.

The regulator's choice of clients is manifested in the decisions it makes. Its desire for survival may at times cause the regulatory agency to make decisions that are not technically optimal. Because the regulator is the state expert in its functional area, it is subject to minimal judicial oversight. Therefore, decision outcomes which are not optimal, and which in some instances are actually inappropriate, may result.

Returning briefly to the notion that planning agencies (including regulators) act as mediators, it is worth noting that the theory of communicative action neglects the organization's response to its environment. Much is said of the control that the planning agency exerts on its clients, but the theory of communicative action seems to suggest that the agency acts as a catalyst. Implicit in this terminology is the notion that the agency itself is not changed by its participation in this process. I contend that the agency *is* affected by its role, and may over time alter its position on important issues. As the organization seeks to reproduce itself, it responds to its environment as necessary to assure its survival.

I do not set out to predict how the regulatory species will evolve from this point. Instead, my objective is to shed some light on the state of the regulatory agency today, to identify the forces that brought it to this point of development, and to demonstrate that these factors may cause the regulator to make nonoptimal (and sometimes, more seriously, inappropriate) decisions. In this chapter, I have tried to accomplish the first two objectives. In the remainder of the book, I shall try to accomplish the third.

Chapter 4

LEGAL ENVIRONMENT OF THE REGULATORY AGENCY

In the preceding chapters, I have attempted to develop my argument that the relationship between the organization and its clients plays a role in public policy outcomes. The previous chapter introduced the notion that the regulatory agency is a special case, and has an unusually broad grant of powers.

The question of judicial oversight plays a small but crucial role in the development of this argument. If the regulatory agency were subject to close and thorough judicial scrutiny of its activities and frequent overturning of its decisions, then there would be less cause for concern about any possible role that the regulator might play. However, this is not the case. Regulatory agencies in general, and the Nuclear Regulatory Commission in particular, have not been subject to intense judicial scrutiny. In fact, judicial oversight of regulatory activities has been largely confined to procedural review. The outcome has been that regulatory agencies have a surprising level of autonomy. In short, what the regulator says usually goes, even after judicial review.

This chapter focuses on the legal framework within which the regulatory agency operates. As I will show, the actors operate within a legal framework that defines and constrains their activities to a great degree. Within those constraints, however, there is a wide range of action lawfully available to the Nuclear Regulatory Commission.

At the heart of this research is the notion that organizations work within boundaries that are defined by some legal enabling framework fashioned by the state to achieve a specific end. A full discussion of whether the framework as designed and implemented achieves its stated goals is another topic for research. However, if one assumes that the judicial system serves as final arbiter of what action best serves state goals, then the absence of substantive judicial review suggests that the regulatory agency itself becomes the de facto arbiter of national goals within its field of technical expertise.

This chapter suggests that the regulatory agency has a high degree of flexibility in its activities, deriving from the agency's role as the expert in the area where it is a regulator. Federal courts, which are charged with the responsibility for reviewing the decisions of regulatory agencies when called upon to do so, base their reviews on due process considerations, rather than on substantive technical evaluations of the agencies' decisions. The courts, then, play the dilettante to the regulatory agencies' expert. As will be shown, the judicial deference to the regulator's expertise was initially an informal, unofficial concession of the judicial system itself. Over time, however, it has become the basic modus operandi of the U.S. judicial system.

The regulatory agency is a special kind of administrative agency. According to Schwartz, the regulatory agency is in a special position because it is vested with a wide range of responsibilities not delegated to other types of agencies. First, the regulatory agency is empowered generally to prescribe what shall or shall not be done in a given situation, as the legislature does. Second, it can determine whether the law has been violated in particular cases and subsequently proceed against violators, as prosecutors and the courts do. And finally, it can impose fines and render what amount to money settlements.[1]

Regulatory powers fall into three broad categories. First is licensing power, the ability to control entry into a given economic activity. This is a power the NRC has, and it is germane to this research. The second power is rate-making, the power to fix rates charged by the companies under the jurisdiction of the agency. Finally, the regulatory agency exercises the authority to approve or prohibit practices employed in business.[2]

This wide grant of power has been delegated to regulatory agencies in response to the concentrated powers of industry. Traditional separation of powers is therefore somewhat lacking in regulatory agencies, as described previously, so that such agencies will have the greatest degree of flexibility possible to carry out their responsibilities.[3]

The history of the regulatory agency in the United States has been one in which a great deal of attention has been given to the independent authority of the regulator, and to assuring that the regulator maintains that authority. The case of *Humphrey's Executor v. the United States* held that the president did not possess unlimited power over members of the Federal Trade Commission (FTC). It held also that the president could not remove

---

[1]   B. Schwartz, *Administrative Law* (Boston: Little, Brown and Co., 1976), p. 5.

[2]   Ibid., p. 12-13.

[3]   Ibid.

members of the commission except "for cause" as specified in the FTC's enabling framework. The result is that the lack of accountability to the White House enables such commissions (of which the NRC is one) to make their own decisions, which may be subject to judicial review, but which are not subject to legal control by the president.[4]

In his discussion of the U.S. legal system, Clark notes the relative autonomy of that system as a whole. He argues that the judicial branch of the government possesses decision-making powers that in effect can be more far-reaching than those of the legislative branch. This power results from the nature of the interaction between the two branches and the consequent oversight authority of the judiciary over the other branches.[5]

Clark argues that "the procedural rules of adjudication cannot be separated from outcomes."[6] He goes on to suggest that even if we assure that the only role of judges is to act within the letter of the law, there still may be significant discretionary judicial authority. The extent of that authority is dependent on the detailed specification of rules.[7]

Similarly, the regulatory agency is also highly autonomous. Its primary source of autonomy derives from its role as expert within its sphere of regulation. Yellin singles out the Nuclear Regulatory Commission in his discussion of the difficulties inherent in the judicial oversight of regulatory agencies, whose activities tend to be technical in nature. Yellin notes that judicial review of administrative decisions of the NRC have two separate elements: procedural and substantive. By procedural review, we mean review to ascertain whether or not the agency has complied with its enabling framework in rendering its decision. By substantive review, we mean review to determine if the decision is the best one on the basis of substantive technical information.[8]

Yellin notes, "If the courts fail to understand the intertwined procedural and technological dimensions of the nuclear power cases, the judicial process becomes a lottery in which outcomes ultimately are determined by intuitive perceptions of the weight of authority rather than by reasoning from evidence."[9]

While suggesting that the judicial review of NRC decisions has been less rigorous than it should have been, Yellin claims that the NRC itself has been ineffective as a regulator because its promotional responsibilities tend

---

[4] Ibid., p. 16.
[5] G.L. Clark, *Judges and the Cities* (Chicago: University of Chicago Press, 1985), p. 40.
[6] Ibid., p. 51.
[7] Ibid., p. 52.
[8] J. Yellin, "High Technology and the Courts: Nuclear Power and the Need for Institutional Reform," *Harvard Law Review*, v. 94, n. 3 (January 1981): 491.
[9] Ibid.

to take precedence over its regulatory functions.[10] Thus, we can infer that the NRC is particularly in need of substantive judicial oversight.

It should be noted that if there is a shortcoming in the judicial review of NRC decisions (and those of other regulatory agencies), it was initially not the result of legal limitations imposed upon the judiciary by Congress. Rather, the limitation to procedural review was self-imposed by the courts, which by tradition demurred to the regulatory agency experts on technical issues. The Administrative Procedure Act (APA) reaffirmed this traditional approach.[11] The APA reasoning argues that if an agency's findings are based on the entire body of evidence before it—including technical evidence—the courts are confined to enforcing procedural fairness and logical consistency with existing statutes.[12]

The underlying logic is twofold. First, the approach recognizes the agency's expertise. Second, it reflects the estimation among judges that their expertise is inadequate to assess technical issues.[13]

The respect for agency expertise has been carried to an extreme in the case of the NRC. The case of *Power Reactor Development Company v. the International Union of Electrical, Radio, and Machine Workers* set a precedent of deference to NRC expertise.[14] This decision has been interpreted in later years to support a finding that the NRC "regulatory scheme . . . is virtually unique in the degree to which broad responsibility is reposed in the administering agency, free of closer prescriptions . . . as to how it shall proceed in achieving statutory objectives."[15] Hence, the scene is set for an NRC with great discretionary power, hardly subject to outside judicial review of its technical decisions.

Yellin claims that the adversarial path to challenging agency decisions helps to expose facts that might otherwise remain hidden if we were to rely on agency expertise alone. In so doing, the process acts as a check on the regulatory agency while legitimating the decision-making process (along with the regulatory agency) by demonstrating public respect for individuals' rights and opinions.[16] This can be perceived as a rephrasing of Weber's basic notion of the organization-client relationship. The regulatory agency gains

---

[10] Ibid., p. 498.

[11] Administrative Procedure Act, sections 551-706, 5 U.S.C. (1946), *United States Code*, 1982, vol. 1: *Organic Laws* (Washington, D.C.: U.S. Government Printing Office, 1983).

[12] Yellin, "High Technology and the Courts," p. 501.

[13] Ibid., p. 503.

[14] 367 U.S. 396 (1961); *Power Reactor Development Co. v. International Union of Electrical, Radio, and Machine Workers, AFL-CIO,* in *Supreme Court Reporter,* v. 81-A (October 1960), pp. 1529-41 (St. Paul, Minn.: West Publishing, 1982).

[15] Yellin, "High Technology and the Courts," pp. 515-16.

[16] Ibid., p. 507.

legitimacy, and thus a continuing raison d'etre, through its contact with individuals (clients). The agency needs its clients.

The adversarial approach has been described by Diver as an incrementalist approach to administrative lawmaking.[17] The author characterizes incrementalism as diffusing conflict by attending in sequence to competing values, as opposed to disposing of conflict by administrative fiat. Rather than sweeping change, the adversarial approach involves a series of conflicts, each resulting in a decision. Taken as a whole, a series of judicial decisions may constitute a sweeping change with important implications for policy implementation down the road. Such change, however, is more commonly associated with major legislation. Diver goes on to express his belief that the incremental method may actually distribute costs and benefits among conflicted parties more efficiently than other means.[18]

The Nuclear Regulatory Commission, then, is an agency that has relatively wide decision-making authority based on both statute and legal precedent. It carries out a large part of its authority through an adversarial process that can be characterized as incremental. Because of its expertise, the NRC's decisions tend to be subjected to judicial review primarily on the basis of procedural compliance. These points are borne out by the Bailly case, which will be discussed in the next chapters.

---

[17] C.S. Diver, "Policymaking Paradigms in Administrative Law," *Harvard Law Review*, v. 95, n. 2 (December 1981): 400.
[18] Ibid.

Part 2

Chapter 5

BACKGROUND: OVERVIEW AND ACTORS

The Indiana Dunes

The Natural Environment

The Bailly controversy unfolds amid the rolling sand hills that are known as the Indiana Dunes. Running the length of the Indiana shoreline of Lake Michigan, the dunes are the product of wind and wave action, and unlike some ocean shorelines that are merely sand-covered bluffs, the dunes are hills of pure sand.

With the passage of time, the rise and fall of the lake has resulted in ridge after ridge of extensive sand dunes. The ridges occasionally trap water, resulting in the unique wetlands associated with the Indiana Dunes. Small lakes, ponds, and bogs are common features. The Indiana Dunes are "living" dunes. The action of wind and wave year in and year out shifts the dunes, creating new ones and eliminating old ones at random. As a result of subtle variations in wind speed and direction, the shape and location of the dunes vary dramatically over time.

The ecology of the dunes is distinctive and was made famous by the work of Henry C. Cowles, who developed his theory of plant succession by observing the dunes ecosystem. Cowles observed that the dunes represented an unusual diversity of flora, ranging from grass species to mature deciduous forest. As he looked more closely, he observed a pattern to the diversity of speciation. Near the shoreline, which was often battered by wind and waves, he observed plants, such as marram grass and sand cherry, that have minimal needs to ensure survival. These simple plants serve to bind together the sand, providing a foothold for later plant life.[1]

---

[1] Henry C. Cowles, "The Physiographic Ecology of Chicago and Vicinity: A Study of the Origin, Development, and Classification of Plant Societies," *Botanical Gazette,* v. 31, n. 3

The foredune area provides protection for the land behind it, which itself was once foredune. This protection makes it possible for plants to decay, promoting the formation of soil. In this relatively enriched environment, needle-leaf trees such as jack pine, white pine, and juniper can thrive. This zone in turn provides protection that makes possible still greater development of soils, which can support more species and denser vegetation. The plant life in this zone includes black oak, white oak, basswood, elm, and sassafras.

Further from the shoreline, cottonwood trees begin to take hold. The cottonwood is more complex and has greater nutrient needs; however, it has the capacity to establish new root systems along its trunk. This is a distinct advantage as more and more sand accumulates around the tree by the continuous action of wind and wave. This system forms the typical components of a foredune area.

Even further inland, away from the lake wind and waves, the dunes support a mature beech-maple climax forest. The length of time necessary to achieve such a forest is estimated at about ten thousand years. The flora in this zone is so dense that oaks and pines cannot survive in its shade. Tulip trees and ferns abound. In the springtime, as the weather warms but before the trees have sprouted leaves, a multitude of spring ephemerals take advantage of the combination of warmth and sunlight so briefly available. Trilliums, jack-in-the-pulpits, and shepherd's purses are just three of the springtime wildflowers gracing the forest floor in this dunal zone.

As Henry Cowles observed this pattern of plant succession, it occurred to him that the pattern that he noted from lakeshore to forest might have greater application. He developed a theory, based on what he saw at the dunes, of plant succession over time, a theory that won broad acceptance as years passed. The dunes continued to play a role in Professor Cowles's work, resulting in his development of the science of ecology in the early 1900s.[2] Cowles Bog, a distinctive wetlands at the Indiana Dunes, was named for him, and acknowledges the innovative nature of his studies.

Past Controversies

The Indiana Dunes have long been acknowledged as an important resource in the region. Industries have settled there to take advantage of the ease of transport that Lake Michigan provides. Private individuals have

---

(1901): 170-77; reprinted in *Ecological Succession*, ed. Frank B. Golley, pp. 23-30 (Stroudsburg, Pa.: Dowden, Hutchinson, and Ross, 1977).

[2]   R.H. Platt, *The Open Space Decision Process*, University of Chicago Department of Geography Research Papers, no. 142 (Chicago: University of Chicago, Department of Geography, 1972), p. 141.

built their homes there to enjoy the great beauty of lake and dunes. Residents of Gary, Chicago, and other nearby cities have visited the dunes in great numbers to enjoy their recreational advantages. Purists have called for preservation of the dunes in their natural state. The multiplicity of land uses to which the dunes have been subject has resulted in a series of controversies over the years.

The primary industrial pressure on the dunes has come from the steel industry. The first mills in the region, the South Works, were built in the 1880s at the mouth of the Calumet River in Illinois, just beyond the western boundary of the dunes.[3]

In 1906, United States Steel Corporation established a major steel-producing facility and a company town in what became Gary, Indiana. The open space between the South Works and the U.S. Steel Facilities quickly filled up. Inland Steel, Youngstown Sheet and Tube, and other heavy industries established major bases of operation in the region. In 1916, Indiana Harbor, an artificial port, opened to serve the transport needs of the Inland and Youngstown operations.[4]

It quickly became apparent that if the dunes were to continue as a recreational and natural resource, quick action was required. Illinois residents (particularly Chicagoans eager for an escape from the city) provided important help in this early effort to preserve the dunes. In 1923, the State of Indiana established the Indiana Dunes State Park, thus protecting just over three miles of prime shoreline from further development.[5]

As time passed, these four competing uses of the dunes (industrial, residential, recreational, and natural) continued to come into conflict. In the late 1950s, the conflict erupted, with the 1958 proposal by the Army Corps of Engineers to create Burns Harbor from a makeshift ditch that was originally dug in 1923 to drain inland marshes for agricultural use.[6]

At that time, the Indiana Dunes State Park accounted for 3.3 miles of shoreline. Three residential communities (Ogden Dunes, Dune Acres, and Beverly Shores) also enjoyed shorelines within the dunes ecosystem. During congressional hearings, these communities were characterized as "among America's finest exclusive communities," because of their elegant vacation and year-round homes.[7]

---

3   H.M. Mayer, "Politics and Land Use: The Indiana Shoreline of Lake Michigan," *Annals of the Association of American Geographers*, v. 54 (December 1964): 508-23.
4   Platt, *The Open Space Decision Process*, p. 14.
5   Ibid.
6   Ibid., p. 147.
7   Ibid., p. 145-47.

Industry continued its hold on the dunes. In addition, the Northern Indiana Public Service Company (NIPSCO) held a Z-shaped tract of land between Ogden Dunes and Dune Acres. The utility would later propose to build its Bailly nuclear generating facility on the site (figure 1).

In an effort to protect the dunes from the immediate pressure of the Burns Harbor project and the long-term pressures that might come from its industrial neighbors, the three residential communities joined together. Their strategy was to establish a national park that would encompass as much of the dunes as possible. Some of the residents were even willing to include their own homesites in the land for the national park, although most were not.

The members of this group were few in number, and given their income levels, they were hardly representative of their county, much less of the Hoosier population in general. They personally stood to gain a great deal from preservation of the dunes. Even so, they were not well united. Many who opposed the advance of industry in the dunes were unwilling to support efforts to establish a national park. Some feared the influx of recreational traffic nearly as much as they did industrial advance. In contrast, the benefits of continued industrial exploitation of the dunes were generally perceived as being widespread. Among those benefits were jobs, tax dollars, and a higher overall standard of living for everyone in the region.

The Save the Dunes Council, as the group came to be known, therefore had great difficulty in building wide support for its cause within the State of Indiana. The members eventually turned to Illinois Senator Paul Douglas for assistance. Reluctant at first, Senator Douglas succumbed to the pleas of the council and to his own memories of the dunes. On Easter evening, 1958, Senator Douglas telephoned the leader of the Save the Dunes Council to let her know that he planned to introduce a bill to establish an Indiana Dunes National Monument.[8] But victory would be hard-won.

In 1959, an unincorporated tract within the dunes ecosystem was incorporated as Portage, Indiana. The city was zoned as industrial, encouraging quick industrial development.[9] National Steel broke ground for a steel finishing plant. NIPSCO began work on a coal-fired electrical generating plant on the site where they would later begin work on the Bailly facility.

This round of development weakened the argument that the dunes constituted an important natural area that should be saved. The council continued its battle over the years, however. In 1962, the battle to save the dunes was struck a heavy blow as the Indiana Port Commission announced

---

[8] J.R. Engel, *Sacred Sands: The Struggle for Community at the Indiana Dunes* (Middletown, Conn.: Wesleyan University Press, 1983), pp. 260-61.

[9] Ibid., p. 262.

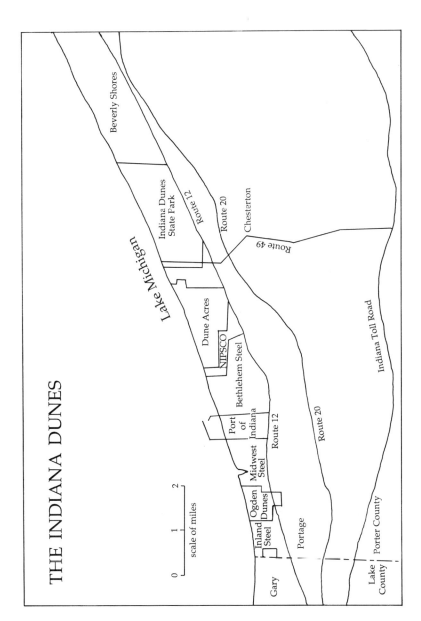

Fig. 1. The Indiana Dunes. The proposed Bailly site is in the Z-shaped parcel owned by NIPSCO.
After Rutherford H. Platt, The Open Space Decision Process: Spatial Allocation of Costs and Benefits. University of Chicago
Department of Geography Research Paper no. 142 (Chicago: University of Chicago Department of Geography, 1972).

that Bethlehem Steel had contracted for the removal of two and one-half million cubic yards of sand from the central dunes area. The sand was taken to Northwestern University in Evanston, Illinois, where it was used as fill for expansion of the campus.[10] At the same time, the Burns Harbor operation continued to loom as a threat.

Eventually, the council was able to rally additional support to its cause. Indiana's Senator Vance Hartke, and the state's new Senator, Birch Bayh, along with congressmen from many other states, came on board. Local and national conservation and civic groups such as the Sierra Club, the National Parks and Conservation Association, the Nature Conservancy and the Izaak Walton League lent their support. Trade unions, educators, and newspapers joined up.

Even with its broadened base of support, it was 1966 by the time a compromise providing for both the Indiana Dunes National Lakeshore and the Port of Indiana at Burns Harbor was passed by Congress. On July 16, 1970, the Port of Indiana officially opened.[11] The Indiana Dunes National Lakeshore was dedicated on September 8, 1972, in the centennial year of the world's first national park, Yellowstone.[12]

Competing uses have consistently been at the heart of dunes controversy. Certainly, economic considerations have formed a major part of the controversy engulfing the dunes, but Engel argues that this is not the only feature of the debate. Engel claims that more personalized attachments to the dunes, an almost spiritual link between the dunes and those who love them, form an important nonquantifiable element of this early controversy. At any rate, it is clear that those who would support the dunes have historically carried on their battles over long periods of time. This was again the case in the controversy over Bailly.[13]

By providing a detailed analysis of a land-use conflict at the dunes within the public-policy arena, this book This research continues and expands on the research of Platt, Mayer, and Engel. Furthermore, inasmuch as this case illustrates the importance of state apparatus in such conflicts, it adds information to the knowledge base.

The Case for the Bailly Case

The controversy surrounding the proposed Bailly nuclear facility at the Indiana Dunes makes an interesting case study that essentially represents a first-step exploration of the influence of clients on public agencies.

---

[10] Engel, *Sacred Sands*, p. 270.

[11] Platt, *The Open Space Decision Process*, p. 172.

[12] Engel, *Sacred Sands*, p. 281.

[13] Ibid.

The nature of the organization-client relationship makes it poorly suited to a statistical analysis, largely because of the difficulty of identifying an appropriate data base. Therefore, a case study is useful for illuminating the general topic.

The historical perspective on the dunes presented above suggests that they are certainly no stranger to battles involving citizens groups and public agencies, and therefore makes the Bailly controversy an enticing case. As evidenced by past controversies centered on the dunes, and a notion echoed by Engel, the parties involved in controversy (or clients, as they will be called in this research) have tended to be both sophisticated and robust. Such sophisticated and robust clients as the industry and private individuals involved in previous dunes battles are relatively even competitors for agency favors. For this reason, I have chosen the Bailly case as a testing ground for my hypotheses on the nature of the organization-client relationship.

The Actors

The Northern Indiana Public Service Company (NIPSCO)

The Northern Indiana Public Service Company traces its ancestry to the organization of the Fort Wayne Gas Light Company in 1853. As settlement in Indiana spread from south to north, the utility's jurisdiction spread. At the end of the 1800s, northwestern Indiana was settled, and heavy industry (including Standard Oil, Inland Steel, and United States Steel) came into the region. This was to have a major influence on the utility.

In 1926, NIPSCO adopted its current organizational structure. Today, NIPSCO is the sole provider of energy (both natural gas and electricity) in twenty-five counties in northern Indiana. Among its customers, however, industries in the region are by far the largest consumers. A representative of the utility estimated that 50 percent of NIPSCO's energy is sold to industry. The major rationale for NIPSCO's choice of the Bailly site was to be near its major consumers. As energy is carried across power lines, losses occur; the shorter the distance the power is carried, the smaller the line losses. From a purely economic perspective, the Bailly site was a good choice for the utility. Unfortunately, the utility failed to predict the concerted efforts that would be exerted to stop the Bailly facility.

Joint Intervenors (JI)

The Joint Intervenors began with the activities of residents of Dune Acres, a community nestled on the shore of Lake Michigan in the midst of the Indiana Dunes. Local individuals, led by Mildred Warner, James

Newman (professor of history and philosophy at Indiana University Northwest), Edward Osann (a patent attorney practicing out of Chicago), and Charlotte and Herbert Reed, donated money and time to win standing to oppose NIPSCO's plan to build the Bailly plant.

Initially, this group, the Concerned Citizens Against Bailly, worked alone, not by choice but of necessity. In the early days, they sought advice in lieu of actual assistance from Businessmen for the Public Interest (BPI—the group is now called Business and Professional People for the Public Interest). The BPI is a not-for-profit organization of public interest attorneys who focus their expertise on environmental issues, particularly antinuclear issues. BPI provided the Concerned Citizens with legal advice on strategies to pursue their own legal battle against Bailly, while BPI's own organizational efforts were focused on another case. During that period, Edward Osann acted as the group's attorney. Beginning about 1975, BPI took over the legal duties, and continued until the battle ended.

The Porter County chapter of the Izaak Walton League was another early participant in the Bailly controversy, although its support was primarily financial. Other groups entered the fray later, after the BPI and the Concerned Citizens had mapped out their strategy of legal challenges.

The Bailly Alliance played a small, though vocal role. As publisher of the *Bailly Alliance News*, the group organized and publicized local outcry against the plant. The opposition by the two locals of the United Steelworkers represents something of a surprise as the group split with local industry management on the issue. The steelworkers maintained that the Bailly plant posed a serious hazard in case of an accident, and that the proposed evacuation plans were unworkable. The City of Gary and the State of Illinois also became involved in the Bailly controversy on grounds of safety. Critical Mass, also listed as a Joint Intervenor, was not important to the controversy.

Early on, the Concerned Citizens had little support outside their own neighborhood. The group concentrated its efforts on raising money to finance its legal battle against the Bailly plant, garnering some support from the Izaak Walton League, as previously mentioned. Throughout most of the group's existence, it worked with little outside support. In the late 1970s, however, additional groups began to join them in their battle. The collective action of these groups began to make the news. Moreover, throughout the United States, similar groups were also picking up steam in a larger collective action against nuclear energy.

The existence of other, unrelated groups fighting battles against other nuclear facilities was helpful to the Concerned Citizens. While they continued their own legal battle, bolstered by the resources (both financial and legal) of BPI, their cause made the news. While the Concerned Citizens remained small and local, NIPSCO seemed willing and able to put up a fight. It was after the power base of the Joint Intervenors swelled and was folded into a larger antinuclear, proenvironmental movement that the utility retreated from battle. The JI had succeeded in stalling construction at Bailly long enough to make it uneconomical for NIPSCO.

The Nuclear Regulatory Commission (NRC)

The Nuclear Regulatory Commission (NRC) began its life in 1946 as the Atomic Energy Commission (AEC). Created by the Atomic Energy Act (Public Law 79-585), the AEC took over responsibility for the research and production facilities where the atomic bomb had been developed during World War II, a responsibility that had been held previously by the Army Corps of Engineers. The infant AEC was given a broader mandate than that previously held by the Army Corps, as development and promotion of peacetime (as well as wartime) uses of atomic power came under its purview.

The Atomic Energy Act of 1946 granted the AEC absolute control over the development and use of atomic energy. The act ordered that the federal government would continue to own all nuclear production facilities and nuclear reactors. Furthermore, all technical information and research results pertaining to atomic energy were to be classified at birth, placed under AEC control, and excluded from the normal application of the patent system.[14]

Initially, the AEC devoted most of its resources to weapons development and production. The organization of the agency was highly decentralized and followed the Army's strategy of using industrial contractors to manage the government-owned facilities. At its birth, the agency had about five thousand employees, supplemented by roughly fifty thousand employees of the AEC's contractors. This ratio remained more or less constant over the agency's life.[15]

The AEC was originally organized into four divisions: research, production (of enriched uranium and plutonium), engineering, and military application. It was also given control of several federal laboratories (including Argonne National Laboratory, outside Chicago) for the development of nuclear power.

In the late 1940s and early 1950s, the AEC used only a small part of its resources to develop power reactors and a good portion of that was for military purposes. Many of these reactors were developed as power sources for

---

[14] R. Civiak, *Nuclear Regulatory Commission Organizational History*, Congressional Research Service (Washington, D.C.: U.S. Government Printing Office, 1982), p. 4.
[15] Ibid.

naval vessels, especially for submarines. Still, the years from 1952 to 1954 saw several prototype nonmilitary reactors put to the test.

In 1955, the AEC launched its first large-scale effort to generate electricity using nuclear power, the Experimental Reactor Program. Under this program, AEC contractors designed, constructed, and operated experimental reactors representing a variety of technological approaches. A sixty-megawatt pressurized water reactor (PWR) built in Shippingport, Pennsylvania, under the terms of this program became the first nuclear power plant in the United States to produce and sell electricity commercially, when the Duquesne Light Company put it on-line in 1957.[16]

Congress moved to revise the Atomic Energy Act in 1954 as a means to encourage the private sector to participate in the development of nuclear energy. The revisions specified: (1) private ownership of nuclear facilities; (2) private use (but not ownership) of nuclear materials; (3) a more liberal patent policy; (4) greater access to information about reactor technology; and (5) the supply of certain AEC services, such as the preparation of reactor fuel, to commercial firms.[17]

These revisions also created a licensing and regulatory system that the AEC would use to oversee the infant nuclear industry in the private sector. (These amendments to the regulatory function of the AEC will be discussed in greater detail later in this chapter.) The AEC continued its control over the government laboratories and thus continued to play a leading role in technology development.

In those early days, the development of nuclear power for electricity production was slow, largely because of market forces. Fossil fuels were relatively cheap and plentiful, while nuclear energy, still in the development stage of the product cycle curve, was relatively expensive and certainly untested. Private industry was not prepared to risk the large sums of money necessary to bring nuclear energy to fruition. It fell to the AEC, therefore, to implement the national goals set by President Eisenhower and Congress for the commercial development of nuclear energy. Thus, the AEC became a promoter of nuclear energy.

The AEC pursued its role as promoter by instituting the Power Demonstration Reactor Program in 1955. Under the terms of this program, the AEC would supply in-kind services for utilities interested in developing nuclear power plants. Whereas the utility would assume the risk of construction, ownership, and operation of a nuclear plant, the AEC would (1) perform agreed-upon research and development without charge at its own laboratories; (2) buy certain economic and technical data from the partici-

---

[16] Ibid., p. 9.
[17] Ibid., p. 10.

pant; and (3) waive the charge for the use of nuclear fuels, which at that time could legally be owned only by the federal government.[18] Under the terms of this program, fifteen commercial reactors were built using eight different reactor designs.

Direct financial aid to utilities from the AEC continued until 1963, when the landmark Oyster Creek Report was published. The Oyster Creek Report was the end product of an economic analysis of alternative power plants performed by the Jersey Central Power and Light Company. On the basis of this analysis, the utility chose to build a nuclear power plant on the basis of economic considerations.[19]

The Oyster Creek Report proved to be a watershed in nuclear power. Before publication of the report, only three utilities had ordered nuclear plants, and then only with a view to being prepared for the future, not for strictly economic reasons. The Oyster Creek Plant was the biggest plant in its day, and the first nuclear plant projected to produce energy at a lower cost than traditional fossil fuel plants.

The publication of the Oyster Creek Report stimulated expansion of the commercial nuclear power industry. In the year the report was published, three other nuclear plants were ordered. Seven were ordered a year later, in 1965. Twenty were ordered in 1966, and thirty in 1967. By the end of 1972, public utilities in the United States had ordered a total of 142 nuclear plants.[20] It was clear that the AEC had performed its promotional responsibilities admirably. It was time for the agency to turn its attention to assuring that the reactors would be operated safely.

Efforts to assure safe operations of nuclear power plants began with revisions of the Atomic Energy Act in 1954, providing for private ownership of nuclear facilities, private use of nuclear fuels and access by the utility industry to the government's technical information.[21] Under the terms of the revisions, the utility wishing to build a nuclear plant was required to go through a two-stage licensing process. The first part of the process required that the utility obtain a construction permit before it could begin to build the plant. Under the second part of the procedure, the utility could begin operation only after the AEC commissioners found that the plant was built in accordance with AEC specifications.

The AEC had the authority to promulgate regulations, standards, and orders "to protect health and minimize danger to life and property."[22]

---

18 Ibid., p. 11.
19 Ibid., p. 13.
20 Ibid., p. 12.
21 Ibid., p. 15.
22 Ibid.

Persons whose interest might be affected by a proposed nuclear facility were entitled to a hearing upon request. Final decisions by the commission were subject to judicial review.

Conflict of Interest

From the time the nuclear power plant began to go into production, conflict-of-interest charges dogged the AEC. In 1956, the AEC ruled favorably on a request to build a nuclear reactor (to be named after Enrico Fermi) about twenty miles from Detroit. The Advisory Committee on Reactor Safeguards (ACRS) disagreed with the AEC that the plant met minimum safety standards and they recommended that the AEC deny the utility's request for a construction permit. (The AEC had established the ACRS in 1947 as a technical review board concerned with the safety of nuclear plants.) The AEC commissioners ignored the ACRS recommendation and issued a conditional construction permit for the Fermi plant in August 1956.[23]

In response to this turn of events, the Congressional Joint Committee on Atomic Energy held extensive hearings on AEC licensing procedures. The committee considered separating the AEC's promotional and regulatory functions at that time, but decided against such a strategy. Congress took action, however, to amend the Atomic Energy Act (Public Law 85-256) to establish the ACRS as an official statutory body responsible for the review of all applications for construction and/or operation of nuclear power plants. The ACRS also assumed responsibility for publishing its findings. In addition, Congress required the AEC commissioners to hold public hearings on all applications for licensing, not only on those that generated formal opposition.[24]

In 1958, the AEC established its Office of the Hearing Examiner, which was designed as a quasi-legal forum for the discussion of particular aspects of specific nuclear plants. Besides providing a forum for public access to the review process, the office also provided a public record attesting to the completeness of the review. Unfortunately, the hearing examiners were trained in law, and not in the technical aspects of nuclear energy. Consequently, their reviews were largely procedural in nature.

To deal with this shortcoming, and to assure a fairer hearing on technical matters, Congress authorized the replacement of the hearing examiners with regional Atomic Safety and Licensing Boards (ASLBs). Each board was to have three members—two with significant technical expertise, one trained in the conduct of hearings. The ASLBs relied upon ACRS reports and recommendations and testimony of AEC staff, the utility, and other

---

[23] Ibid., p. 16.
[24] Ibid.

parties with an interest in the proceedings (called intervenors) to make their decisions.[25] The commissioners of the AEC were responsible for overseeing the regional ASLBs.

Another layer was added to the AEC in 1969, when the regional Atomic Safety and Licensing Appeal Boards (ASLABs) were established. The ASLABs took responsibility for reviewing decisions of the ASLBs. The AEC commissioners retained responsibility for oversight of the ASLABs. The entire process was subject to outside judicial review.

The National Environmental Policy Act

It is important to remember that the AEC has never operated in a public policy vacuum. This became clear with the passage of the National Environmental Policy Act of 1969 (NEPA: Public Law 91-190), which would profoundly change the mandate of the AEC.

Initially, the AEC ruled that it need not consider radiological impacts of nuclear plants under NEPA regulations, claiming that it already considered such impacts under its own regulations. The AEC further ruled that its only responsibility in nonnuclear environmental matters was to ensure that another appropriate agency had certified that an applicant for a license had complied with that other agency's standards.

On the basis of this interpretation, the AEC refused to hear intervenors' arguments concerning the potential for thermal pollution resulting from a nuclear plant proposed for a location near Calvert Cliffs, Maryland. The intervenors appealed the AEC's decision to the U.S. Court of Appeals, which ruled against the AEC in July 1971 and required that the AEC comply with NEPA in addition to its own regulations.[26] The AEC 1972 *Annual Report* discussed the changing mission of the AEC.[27] Beginning that year, in response to President Nixon's Energy Message, Congress authorized the AEC to undertake research and development on "the preservation and enhancement of a viable environment."[28] Whereas before, the AEC had been responsible for safeguarding against radiation damage, this new direction gave the agency responsibility for the full range of environmental consequences of nuclear plant construction and operation.

Still, charges of conflict of interest dogged the AEC. Over the years, Congress pursued several unsuccessful efforts to disband the AEC. Then, in 1974, critics of the dual-responsibility AEC were successful at last. In that

---

[25] Ibid., p. 17.

[26] Atomic Energy Commission, *1972 Annual Report to Congress* (Washington, D.C.: U.S. Government Printing Office, 1973).

[27] Civiak, *Nuclear Regulatory Commission Organizational History*, p. 19.

[28] Ibid., p. 21.

year, the Energy Reorganization Act carved the AEC's promotion and regulatory functions into two separate duties within two separate agencies. Since then, the Energy Research and Development Administration (ERDA) has had sole responsibility for promoting nuclear energy. The AEC's regulatory functions passed on to the Nuclear Regulatory Commission, which continues to be responsible for licensing nuclear power plants. Along with responsibility for licensing procedures, the NRC inherited the ASLB, the ASLAB, and the AEC commission as its head, thus preserving the licensing procedures developed and used by the AEC since the mid-1950s.[29]

The Impact of Three Mile Island on the NRC

The accident at Three Mile Island in 1979 was another event that had a major impact on the NRC, especially at the top administrative levels. The TMI accident focused nationwide attention on the risks of nuclear energy. Three independent studies of NRC performance in the accident noted a need to strengthen management authority within the commission. In 1980, a plan to reorganize the NRC to increase the management authority of the NRC's chairman went into effect. This action was intended to minimize the confusion of commission decisions by making its chairperson ultimately responsible for the actions of the NRC.

The long history of the NRC, then, begins with the birth of an agency (the AEC) designed primarily to promote the commercial production and use of nuclear energy. This promotional aspect of the agency's responsibilities dominated its activities through most of the 1960s. Only after growing public sentiment in favor of protecting the environment and subsequent passage of the National Environmental Policy Act of 1969 did the AEC begin to concentrate on its regulatory functions. Finally, amidst conflict-of-interest charges, the AEC was restructured, emerging as two separate agencies, each responsible for one important—but inherently distinct—function.

Within this history lie the seeds of this research. What pressures are brought to bear on the agency as it makes its decisions? How does the agency cope with its dual role—and with its separate clients? Do outside influences play a role? The next chapter provides a glimpse of the answers to these questions by reviewing the decisions of the AEC/NRC in the case of the Bailly nuclear power plant.

These, then are the actors: the NRC, NIPSCO, and the Joint Intervenors. The battleground was primarily the administrative courts of the NRC. To an extent, the battle was also fought in the streets, although early public sentiment favored NIPSCO and its Bailly plant. In the end, it was a war of attrition.

---

29 Ibid., p. 20.

Chapter 6

THE BAILLY DECISIONS

The Bailly Controversy

The Bailly controversy began on August 20, 1970, when the Northern Indiana Public Service Company (NIPSCO) applied to the Atomic Safety and Licensing Board (ASLB) of the Atomic Energy Commission for permission to build a 685 megawatt boiling water reactor on a Z-shaped tract of land it owned. This site, named for Joseph Bailly, an early homesteader in the area, was bounded on the north by Lake Michigan, on the west by the Bethlehem Steel plant, and on the south and east by the Indiana Dunes National Lakeshore (IDNL). Within the boundaries of the IDNL, also to the east of the NIPSCO property, was the town of Dune Acres, a residential area. As previously noted, the multiplicity of land uses has been a source of periodic conflict among those who use (or would use) the shoreline of Lake Michigan for their own purposes.

When word of NIPSCO's permit request became public, the familiar pattern of conflict repeated itself. As in the debate over creation of a national park versus construction of a harbor at the dunes, the conflict was played out in a public policy forum. In the Bailly case, however, the forum was provided not by Congress, but by the U.S. Atomic Energy Commission and its descendent, the Nuclear Regulatory Commission. The bureaucratic nature of that forum played a role in the outcome of the case.

The AEC/NRC, like other bureaucratic organizations, is subject to pressure and possible capture by its clients and potential clients. In the Bailly case, there were two client groups, each desiring an outcome directly opposed to the other: NIPSCO wanted to build a nuclear facility on the Bailly site; the Joint Intervenors objected.

During the course of the Bailly controversy, which extended until mid-1982, the AEC/NRC changed its organizational mission. Construction of NIPSCO's Bailly facility was undoubtedly consistent with the AEC's mission to promote the use of nuclear power for peacetime uses. However, the NRC's organizational mission, to regulate the nuclear industry as a means to guard the public health against nuclear dangers, seemingly put the NRC at odds with the utility. At the same time, the goal of the JI seemed to be in line with the NRC's organizational mission.

To the extent that an organization can choose its client, a plausible choice for an organization would be the client that most closely represents the organizational mission of the agency. In the Bailly case, then, the expectation would be that the AEC would render decisions that favored NIPSCO —and thereby promote nuclear energy. The NRC, with a vastly different mission, would be expected to render decisions that reflected concern for public health and the environment, regardless of the effect of its decisions on the ability of the utility to proceed with its plans to build the plant. Furthermore, one would also expect that to ensure public health and well-being, the NRC would strictly enforce its rules for determining site suitability.

On the other hand, the AEC/NRC might choose its client on the basis of other considerations. An important consideration might be its historical relationship with NIPSCO. The AEC had long experience in dealing with public utilities, and from 1970 (and perhaps earlier) to 1974 was in contact with NIPSCO concerning the Bailly facility. Staffers within the agency and the utility might well have established a close working relationship that could later work to the benefit of the utility. The JI, having no reason for interaction with the NRC, clearly had no way of developing a similar relationship. If history played a role, then the NRC's decisions would be expected to further NIPSCO's organizational goal of building the Bailly facility.

The query described above essentially asks whether the agency follows its own organizational mission as determined by its enabling framework or relies on historical links. In either case, the ultimate goal is organizational survival. In acting on its organizational mission, the agency would seem to seek continued support from its creator, Congress. If acting on the basis of a historical relationship, the agency would seem to rely on its client's continuing good will for survival. In both instances, the agency seeks legitimacy, the key to survival.

The clients, too, rely on their ability to appear legitimate as a means to enter the process. For NIPSCO, making a case for legitimacy was easy: as a formal legal creation of the State of Indiana, legitimacy was automatic. The JI, on the other hand, had a more difficult case: to be granted standing to confront the utility in the NRC's administrative court, they had first to provide strong evidence that they spoke on behalf of a legitimate public interest. This they were able to do and thus became an actor in the Bailly case.

Each source of client legitimacy carries with it the potential for organizational influence. While NIPSCO had a legal mandate, the JI had (or claimed to have) a public mandate. To the extent that such mandates translate into legitimacy, and to the extent that the organization can draw on its client's legitimacy to enhance its own legitimacy, the organization can improve its own chances for survival. The Bailly case represents an interplay among the factors described above: organizational mission, historical relationships, and legal and public mandates.

NIPSCO's request for permission to build a nuclear generating facility on its Bailly site met quick opposition from the Joint Intervenors. A group of Dune Acres residents, calling themselves the Concerned Citizens Against Bailly Nuclear Station, began immediately to organize opposition to the facility. Their early efforts focussed on fund-raising within the group. Their goal was to establish a fund large enough to enable them to wage the legal war that they knew lay ahead.

One of their members, Edward Osann, a patent attorney with an office in Chicago's Loop, took on the role of legal advisor. Quickly, he moved to contact the Businessmen for the Public Interest (BPI), a nonprofit organization that provides legal counsel to antinuclear efforts. Already involved in another case, BPI was unable to help the Concerned Citizens outright. The businessmen did, however, provide advice and moral support in those early days. BPI advised the Concerned Citizens to raise as much money as possible and, if outright victory seemed impossible, to seek delays.

Early on, the Concerned Citizens seemed to be in trouble. Unable to gain full assistance from BPI, Osann was forced to continue as the standard-bearer in the legal fight against the Bailly facility. He took time from his own practice to pursue the Bailly case in the administrative courts of the NRC.

Financial assistance was also hard to come by in the early days of the conflict. The Concerned Citizens went back time and time again to their neighbors in Dune Acres for more money, and eventually, the group wore out its welcome. However, the Izaak Walton League was a frequent contributor to the fund and on several occasions bailed out the Concerned Citizens with infusions of money.

For its part, NIPSCO was determined to build its nuclear facility on the Bailly site. After all, it was their land. The site was a good choice from the utility's perspective. With half of its energy going to the heavy industries along the lakeshore, this site would minimize line losses and thereby improve NIPSCO's profit margin. The utility owned other land some distance from Lake Michigan, and so could have chosen a site elsewhere for its nuclear facility. But the NRC had granted a construction permit for

NIPSCO's nuclear generating facility at the Bailly site. Why, then, should the utility not build the facility on its first-choice site?

The permit grant did not daunt the Concerned Citizens. Having won standing to oppose the utility in the NRC's administrative courts, the Joint Intervenors (as they were now officially known) settled in for a long, hard battle to assure that NIPSCO would not build its nuclear generating facility on the Bailly site. Ever hopeful of gaining support for their position, the Joint Intervenors continued their efforts to gain media attention, public support, and funds for their cause. In the meantime, Osann pursued their case before the NRC.

What the JI lacked in money and public support, they made up with persistence and sophistication in their legal battle. Again and again they went before the NRC, challenging the Bailly site directly and indirectly. The JI's direct challenges focused on the substantive issues, providing evidence of environmental degradation and public safety hazards resulting from the construction. Their indirect challenges focused on procedural aspects of the case, and centered on the failure of the NRC to comply with the agency's own procedures and legal mandate as required by its enabling legislation.

Although the Joint Intervenors challenged the Bailly site (either directly or indirectly) before the NRC nearly thirty times, they were not successful in putting a halt to the facility through administrative challenges. No NRC decision revoked the utility's construction permit. However, in 1982, NRC decisions notwithstanding, the JI had their way. A combination of economic factors, including rising construction costs, growing concern over nuclear energy resulting from the Three Mile Island accident, and a decline in the fortunes of heavy industry in northwestern Indiana, forced NIPSCO to abandon the Bailly facility. The NRC allowed the utility to withdraw its request to build the Bailly plant "without prejudice." This stipulation meant that the NIPSCO's option to apply for a new building permit at a later date was not foreclosed. (Realistically speaking, it is highly unlikely that the utility would reconsider a nuclear facility at the Bailly site in the near future.) The NRC's final decision in the case required NIPSCO to return the Bailly site to its original condition.

Was Bailly an Appropriate Site?

A salient feature of the Bailly case is that there is strong evidence to suggest that the site violated the NRC's own rules for facility siting. A study carried out by Richard Hansis, associate professor of geography at Valparaiso University in northwest Indiana, indicated that the facility's safety zones had been calculated by a method that considerably misrepresented the area's population densities. In order to meet the low level of population density required for a construction permit, the NRC had allowed NIPSCO to include a sizable portion of Lake Michigan in the concentric rings used for their calculations. (Figure 2 shows how the methodology was flawed. Table 1 represents the same basic data.)

Moreover, Hansis discovered, the measurement of distance from the Bailly site to population centers in the region also appeared to be questionable. According to an NRC statement, the distances used officially to calculate the mileage between the Bailly site and population centers were "merely approximately deduced from large scale maps. . . . The reference points or boundaries [were] not known."[1] Hansis refers to the measurement system as "rubber yardsticks." Table 2 shows how the distances used by NIPSCO and approved by the NRC compare with more carefully measured distances. The distance between Bailly and Gary, as measured by NIPSCO and approved by the NRC, is ten miles. The correct distance is half that, five miles. Three locations that are actually adjacent to the proposed Bailly facility (Dune Acres, Bethlehem Steel, and the Indiana Dunes National Lakeshore) are listed by NIPSCO/NRC at anywhere from one to four and one-half miles away from the site.

The U.S. Department of the Interior (DOI) had additional problems with the site and entered the case as a friend of the court. The DOI contended that construction at the Bailly site was harming Cowles Bog, an important wetland at the dunes. Each month, DOI submitted a report in which its author, Mark Reshkin, professor of geology at Indiana University Northwest, chronicled the dewatering caused by construction at Bailly.

Without defensible evidence that the Bailly site was inappropriate, the decisions by the NRC would carry significant weight because of the agency's expertise. Consequently, it would be impossible to draw any conclusions whatsoever about the case. Without evidence questioning NRC decisions, we would find ourselves as researchers deferring to agency expertise on the substantive issue of the case.

Presentation of this evidence is intended to stimulate questioning of NRC decisions. If, as the evidence suggests, the Bailly site was inappropriate on the basis of substantive considerations, then on what basis did the NRC make its decisions reaffirming the site? This research argues that the NRC's clients played a role in the decisions. Specifically, the NRC's decisions reflect the agency's concern for survival. As a result, I argue, the NRC decisions favored the client that the agency perceived to be stronger and thus more helpful in its quest for survival.

---

1   R. Hansis, "Emergency Planning and Nuclear Power Plant Siting in Northwest Indiana," paper presented at the Annual Meeting of the Association of American Geographers, Louisville, Ky., in (April 1980): 5.

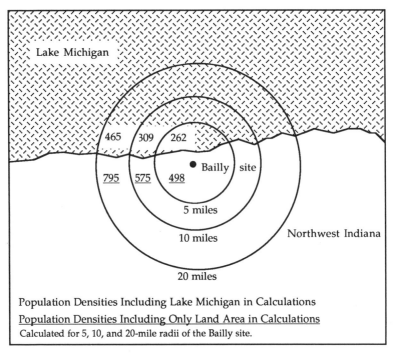

Fig. 2. *Population Densities Calculated with and without Lake Michigan for the Proposed Bailly Nuclear Generating Facility.*

TABLE 1: Population density figures for siting Bailly.

Radial distance	Population 1970	Density: NRC/NIPSCO method[a]	Density: Hansis method[b]	Siting criteria maximums
0-5mi.	20,512	262	498	100
5-10mi.	71,088	309	575	150
10-20mi.	438,400	465	795	400
20-30mi.	1,670,000	591	891	----

[a] Includes Lake Michigan in the circumferential distance.
[b] Excludes Lake Michigan from the circumferential distance.

TABLE 2: Deduced and measured distances (in miles) from the proposed Bailly site.

Place	Deduced	Measured
Gary	10.0	5.0
Portage	4.5	1.0
Dune Acres	2.0	adjacent
Porter	3.25	1.25
Burns Harbor	2.5	1.5
Bethlehem Steel plant	1.0	adjacent
Midwest Steel plant	4.5	2.0
Indiana Dunes National Lakeshore	4.5	adjacent

SOURCE: Hansis, "Emergency Planning," p. 5.

The Case Study

What follows is a chronology of the decisions in the Bailly case.[2] By and large, the decisions were precipitated by challenges by the Joint Intervenors. The individual actions include both procedural and substantive claims. For the most part, the NRC's decisions favored NIPSCO. Each such decision can therefore be viewed as a reaffirmation of the Bailly site. Conversely, no decision prohibited the utility from locating its nuclear facility at this contentious site.

Although the JI were united on the issue of the Bailly facility, they were not united on any other issue, nor in their stated organizational missions. For example, the mission of the labor unions is to advance the economic goals of their members. The Izaak Walton League is concerned about all aspects of environmental degradation. The Critical Mass Energy Project is founded on the belief that nuclear energy should be opposed wherever it is found. The Lake Michigan Federation is committed to the health and well-being of Lake Michigan. In spite of these differences in their organizational goals, they constituted a unified opposition to the Bailly facility.

----

[2] Please note that the decisions cited are identified by their NRC reference numbers (i.e., ALAB 239, CLI-73-26, and LPB-74-82). The documents from which the decisions are taken are: (1) Atomic Energy Commission, *Opinions and Decisions* (Washington, D.C.: U.S. Government Printing Office) annual (hereafter called AEC, *Opinions*); and (2) Nuclear Regulatory Commission. *Issuances: Opinions and Decisions of the Nuclear Regulatory Commission with Selected Orders* (Washington, D.C.: U.S. Government Printing Office) annual (hereafter called NRC, *Issuances*).

Even though these groups did not possess the statutory legitimacy that NIPSCO enjoyed as a formal creation of the State of Indiana, both administrative and federal courts granted them standing to sue NIPSCO over Bailly. This grant of standing came even though the JI were in little, if any, danger of suffering physical harm as a result of the construction at the Bailly site. Schwartz emphasizes that the easing of requirements for the grant of standing makes it possible for those who have not suffered physical or economic harm to win the right to sue on the basis of aesthetic and environmental well-being as well.[3] He cites a Supreme Court decision that held that "the fact that particular environmental interests are shared by the many rather than the few does not make them less deserving of legal protection through the judicial process."[4]

The JI, then, can be seen to gain legitimacy on the basis of their efforts to advance "particular environmental interests . . . shared by the many." In this respect, they speak on behalf of a legitimate public interest.

The JI used their standing well, bringing NIPSCO before the NRC's administrative courts time and again. In the end, NIPSCO terminated construction at the Bailly site, thus surrendering in this war of attrition. The JI waged their legal attack on two separate grounds: procedural (administrative) and substantive (environmental). Their earliest battles were largely procedural, while the battles waged after NIPSCO received its license to build Bailly were based predominantly on substantive objections. Their final battles combined both strategies.

Permit Application

On August 24, 1970, the Northern Indiana Public Service Company applied to the Atomic Safety and Licensing Board (ASLB) of the AEC to build a 685 megawatt boiling water reactor at its Bailly site, located on the southern shore of Lake Michigan, in Westchester Township, Porter County, Indiana. Following AEC procedures, NIPSCO submitted its environmental report on January 7, 1971. The draft Environmental Impact Statement (EIS) was submitted in July of 1972, with the final EIS following in February of the next year.

---

3   B. Schwartz, *Administrative Law* (Boston: Little, Brown and Co., 1976), pp. 472-73.

4   *Sierra Club v. Rogers C.B. Morton, Individually and as Secretary of the Interior of the United States, et al.,* in *Supreme Court Reporter,* v. 92-A (October 1971): 1361-78 (St. Paul, Minn.: West Publishing, 1974).

Conflict of Interest

Even before the AEC had a chance to rule on NIPSCO's application, the Joint Intervenors went before the Atomic Safety and Licensing Appeals Board (ASLAB) to protest the presence of one of the members of the ASLB, and to request that he be disqualified from the board (ALAB-76).[5]

The JI based their request for Dr. Harry Foreman's disqualification on two separate grounds. The first concerned a possible conflict of interest. The JI claimed that Foreman had served as a consultant to the Northern States Power Company from 1969 through 1971, a period when Northern States was involved in a contentious application for a nuclear plant operating license. Because of this prior relationship, the JI questioned Foreman's ability to carry out his responsibilities in an objective manner.

In its decision, the ASLAB noted that Foreman had never been involved with NIPSCO, adding that when he had consulted with Northern States, he had not, in fact, participated in any hearings before the AEC pertaining to the case. Rather, his consultation was limited to technical matters and to conducting a course on the biological effects of radiation. The board therefore ruled that there was no basis for the JI's conflict-of-interest charge.

The JI's second challenge centered on Foreman's qualifications to serve as a technical member of the ASLB, charging that he possessed no expertise or experience in environmental science or technology. On this challenge, the ASLAB noted that the NRC itself makes appointments to its boards and had in fact appointed Foreman to the ASLB. Therefore, the commission implicitly found that Foreman's educational and professional preparation qualified him to serve on the boards. The appeals board therefore refused to review Foreman's qualifications and ruled against the JI.

Two years later, the JI brought a second motion to the ASLB to have Foreman disqualified, again on grounds of conflict of interest and inadequate qualifications. In the months since the original challenge, the JI noted that Foreman had been absent from many hearings. They charged that his absences had precipitated prejudicial errors in the hearings and had brought into question his credibility. (Foreman's absences also precipitated challenges to the AEC's quorum rules, discussed later in this chapter.) The ASLB ruled that no prejudicial error had resulted from Foreman's absences, reiterated the board's earlier defense of him, and again ruled against the JI. It is worth noting that Harry Foreman, as a sitting member of the ASLB, was involved in this decision (LBP-74-80).

The decision was referred to the appeals board. It was the ASLAB's "customary practice . . . to act upon such referrals on the basis of the papers

---

5   AEC, *Opinions*, 1974, p. 809.

filed, without calling for further briefing or argument."[6] The appeals board reaffirmed the decision of the ASLB (ALAB-239).

Coercion of Witness

On September 8, 1973, the Joint Intervenors submitted to the ASLB a Motion for Order to Show Cause Why Applicant Should Not be Held in Contempt, or in the Alternative for a Protective Order. The JI presented affidavits alleging that an associate of NIPSCO had attempted to coerce one of the JI's witnesses. NIPSCO responded to the motion by arguing that the alleged coercion was "in no way associated with them." The matter was referred to the AEC commissioners, who issued a memorandum and order on October 9, 1973 (CLI-73-26).

The memorandum and order noted the seriousness of the charges: "Coercion of a prospective witness threatens not only the individual in question, but also the integrity of the administrative process itself. All parties have the right to present their cause without intimidation or fear of reprisal. All cases must be heard and evaluated in an open atmosphere free from fear. Petitioners' allegations, if true, are thus of the utmost gravity."[7]

The commissioners referred the matter to the FBI. The administrative record is devoid of any further reference to the coercion issue.

Bailly Construction Permit Approved

Finally, on March 20, 1974, an initial decision on NIPSCO's application came down. The ASLB determined that NIPSCO had satisfied all administrative requirements and approved the permit, provided that the applicant agreed to monitoring of the site for environmental purposes. On April 5, 1974, the board issued the construction permit for the Bailly plant.

Request for Stay

Less than one week after the permit was issued, the JI filed a motion by telegraph. They had two requests. First, they asked that the ASLB stay construction at the Bailly site pending the outcome of their appeal of the permit decision. Second, the JI asked for an extension until April 29, 1974, to give themselves adequate time to prepare and file their exceptions to the permit grant (ALAB-192).

According to the criteria established by the Court of Appeals of the District of Columbia Circuit, the JI could win a stay only if they could show

---

6   AEC *Opinions*, 1975, p. 836.
7   Ibid.

the following: (1) that they were likely to prevail on the merits of their appeal; (2) that without the stay, the JI would be irreparably injured; (3) that issuing the stay would not substantially harm other parties in the proceeding; and (4) that JI's position would serve the public interest.

The ASLAB ruled that the JI had not satisfied the above conditions. They agreed, however, that the situation warranted further research, and granted a temporary emergency stay and extension. The board directed the JI to serve and file a memorandum in support of their motion for a stay pending appeal by April 19, 1974. That memorandum was required to address the four conditions listed above. The board extended the deadline for filing exceptions to the permit to April 29.

On April 30, 1974, the ASLAB considered the previous ruling. They noted that the stay was granted under the assumption that immediate construction activities would result in unintended drainage of wetlands at the dunes. NIPSCO explained that none of its planned construction activities in the initial four months were expected to affect the water table at the dunes. In light of this information, the ASLAB (1) vacated the emergency stay, and (2) denied the JI's request for a stay pending appeal. For its part, NIPSCO was ordered not to undertake any construction that would affect the water table until after September 1, 1974. The board set new deadlines for filing exceptions and briefs (ALAB-200).

The JI replied to this decision by requesting again that the ASLAB reinstate the temporary stay of construction, and asking that the appeals board clarify its order of April 30. The ASLAB responded by reiterating its order preventing NIPSCO from proceeding with any construction activities that would result in dewatering of the dunes. While the JI questioned the lack of monitoring of this order, the ASLAB maintained that it had no reason to assume that NIPSCO would not act in good faith. The board reminded JI that, as a condition for its permit, it had required NIPSCO to establish a groundwater monitoring program (ALAB-201). Denying the stay, the appeals board reiterated its position that the arrangement described above was adequate to protect the dunes—and the interest of the JI.

Before two weeks had passed, the JI had requested another extension of the deadline for filing their brief (from May 21 to June 15). The JI had filed 500 exceptions to the initial permit decision. Not surprisingly, NIPSCO opposed the extension (ALAB-204). In making its decision, the ASLAB noted that "the Intervenors are represented here by counsel who tried the case and who is perforce familiar with that record, having but recently submitted more than 150 pages of proposed findings of fact and conclusions of law to the trial board."[8] In spite of apprehensions over its potentially prejudicial effect on NIPSCO, the ASLAB granted the JI an extension.

In a second motion filed at the same time, the JI suggested that the AEC staff members had acted as "de-facto counsel" for NIPSCO.[9] The ASLAB believed that the JI made the charge because the agency had failed to grant a further extension of time to prepare and file a brief. In its decision the board said, "The gratuitous comment of intervenors' counsel was not only unwarranted but unprofessional. . . . Name calling adds nothing to the stature of counsel or to the merits of his argument."[10]

On May 20, 1974, the ASLAB denied another motion by the JI specifically to prohibit NIPSCO from beginning any construction activities that might lead to dewatering of the dunes area until after September 1, 1974. In so doing, it noted that NIPSCO was already "under an affirmative mandate to do nothing which might lower the water table."[11] The ASLAB reiterated that it had no reason to suspect that NIPSCO would disobey the mandate.

The JI asked for permission to file a supplemental brief in support of their exceptions to the initial decision issued by the licensing board on April 5, 1974. The appeals board noted that it had already granted the JI two extensions. In denying the third extension, the ASLAB's decision is rife with exasperation. "There inevitably comes a point, however, when considerations of the orderly course of the particular proceeding at bar demand that the line be drawn on further retreat from the enforcement of the conditions imposed in prior order. In this instant, that point manifestly has been reached."[12] The appeals board denied the JI motion (ALAB-215).

NIPSCO Files a Motion

On June 4, 1974, the ASLAB ruled on a motion filed by NIPSCO asking the AEC to strike certain of the JI's exceptions and a portion of their brief for failure to comply with the AEC's rules of practice. NIPSCO further asked that the JI be prohibited from filing any additional briefs (ALAB-207).

The appeals board's decision agreed that the briefs in question were imperfectly drawn, but they refused to strike them because the briefs disclosed "the substance of the intervenors' objections with reasonable particularity."[13] On the second motion, the ASLAB acknowledged that the JI were

---

[8] Ibid.
[9] Ibid., p. 837.
[10] Ibid.
[11] Ibid., p. 839.
[12] Ibid., p. 1011.
[13] Ibid., p. 958.

permitted to file no more briefs. The appeals board further pointed out that the JI had not indicated an intent to do so, and it declined to assume that the JI planned to disobey AEC rules. The tone of this decision is roughly analogous to the May 17, 1974, ASLAB decision that favored NIPSCO. In that case, the JI had asked the board to prohibit NIPSCO in advance from disobeying AEC rules prohibiting the utility from beginning construction that might dewater the dunes. In both cases, the party bringing the motion implied that its adversary was acting in bad faith. Likewise in both cases, the board continued to assume good faith and denied the motions.

Quorum

In August, the ASLAB ruled on appeals of two separate permit grants, the Bailly construction permit and an operating permit for the Zion, Illinois, plant. Both appeals were based on charges that AEC quorum rules for members of the ASLB had not been met (ALAB-222).

AEC quorum rules required that at least two of the three members be present at each hearing and that one of the members be qualified in the conduct of administrative proceedings. The appeals board ruled that while the ASLB had complied with the letter of the law, there had been excessive absences of technical members of the board. The board outlined more stringent procedures to help assure that the spirit of the quorum rule be carried out in future hearings. The board refused, however, to rescind the permits, on the basis of challenges to the quorum rule.

Later, the JI brought this issue to the attention of the AEC commissioners, who echoed the ASLAB's concern about possible abuses of the quorum rule. They agreed that the rule required tightening and ruled that all future absences of technical members be explained in the official record. They left implementation procedures to the licensing board. The commissioners, like the appeals board, refused to act retroactively on the quorum rules. Thus the permit for Bailly, along with that for Zion, stood (CLI-74-35).

Stay Expires

Finally, on August 29, 1974, the Atomic Safety and Licensing Appeals Board made a decision on the JI's original challenge to NIPSCO's permit to build the Bailly facility. The board ruled that NIPSCO had complied with the procedural requirements of the AEC and NEPA, and that the plant, as designed, posed no significant threat to the dunes. The ASLAB reaffirmed its initial decision on the permit and allowed its previously ordered partial stay of construction of Bailly to expire (ALAB-224).

The JI responded immediately with two motions before the ASLAB. First, they asked that the appeals board remand the cause for further hearing on the basis of newly discovered evidence. Second, they asked for a stay of the ASLAB decision while they pursued an appeal in the federal courts for further relief.

The JI based their request to remand on their discovery that NIPSCO had contracted to buy a 20 percent share of a planned nuclear facility in Madison, Indiana. The facility, called Marble Hill, was scheduled to begin operation in the early 1980s; like Bailly, it has since been terminated. The JI claimed that with the purchase of this power, the Bailly plant might be unnecessary. The ASLAB ruled that the purchase would not eliminate the need for Bailly. Apparently, the testimony of one of the JI's own witnesses conceding that the capacity added by Bailly would be needed by 1980 did not help their cause. The ASLAB ruled against remanding.

The board likewise ruled against the JI's request for a stay, noting that NIPSCO had made it clear that it had no plans to "undertake prior to October 1, 1974 the construction activities which intervenors allege will have an immediate environmental impact on the Indiana Dunes National Lakeshore."[14]

The Slurry Wall

The next series of actions by the JI concerned the construction of a slurry wall to provide additional environmental protection against the dewatering of the dunes. Originally, NIPSCO had proposed to drain its building site to keep it dry. The utility later proposed to build a slurry wall between its site and the dunes in order to prevent dewatering the dunes at the same time. During the first part of October, the NRC Board of Commissioners issued, *sua sponte*, a decision to call for an "expedited limited hearing [on] the environmental effects, if any, of the slurry wall."[15] The ASLB was given responsibility for holding the hearing (CLI-74-39).

Five days later, the JI contacted the chairman of the ASLB to ask him to arrange a conference call between the JI, the board members, and NIPSCO. The call was placed that evening (LPB-74-82).

The JI asked that the board order NIPSCO to fill in the construction excavation that had occurred up to that point so that the excavation would be above the level of the groundwater table. The JI based their motion on testimony by NRC staff witness Lewis G. Hulman, who indicated that with the excavation at the plant site below the water table, the increased evaporation caused by the open construction could have an adverse impact on the groundwater level at the dunes. The JI claimed that NIPSCO had misrepre-

---

14   Ibid., p. 417.
15   Ibid., p. 631.

sented the situation when it maintained that the construction level would not be below the level of the water table.

As expected, NIPSCO opposed the motion. They countered the JI's argument by reasoning that if their construction was below the water table, it was because of a naturally occurring increase in the level of the water table itself caused by precipitation. NIPSCO further maintained that given the order from the NRC Board of Commissioners for a limited hearing on slurry wall construction, the ASLB did not have jurisdiction to rule on the JI's motion to stop construction.

In ruling on the motion, the board suggested an alternative interpretation of Hulman's testimony. The ASLB suggested that the dewatering, which Hulman had concluded was "an alleged adverse impact relating to construction of the slurry, was in fact an effect resulting from the stay of construction of the slurry wall. The implicit argument is that if the slurry wall were in place, the water would not go into the construction area and there would be no resultant reduction in the groundwater level."[16]

The ASLB declined to act on the JI's oral motion, which they denied without prejudice, leaving open the door for the JI to resubmit their motion in writing.

The next day, the JI brought this same motion before the ASLAB. The appeals board directed all the parties involved to visit the construction site together on Saturday, November 9, 1974, to determine whether the excavation might be drawing down the water table at the dunes. On the basis of that visit, the ASLAB ordered an evidentiary hearing to be held in Chicago on the following Monday (November 11).

Prior to the hearing, on Sunday evening, NIPSCO initiated a conference call to propose a settlement. While maintaining that its construction was not creating a negative impact on the National Lakeshore, NIPSCO offered to accept a recommendation of the AEC staff that they supplement the existing water in the excavation site so as not to dewater Cowles Bog. The JI refused this conference and settlement, and the hearing proceeded as scheduled (ALAB-241).

During the hearing, Hulman (whose testimony had inspired the JI to pursue this line of action) and several other witnesses gave testimony. The JI did not present any positive evidence in their behalf, but they did cross-examine the witnesses extensively. On the basis of the evidence disclosed at the hearing, the ASLAB found that the excavation did not threaten the water table in any areas outside the Bailly construction site. The appeals board refused to grant the JI's motion.

---

16 Ibid., p. 883.

In a memorandum dated November 13, 1974, the appeals board re-affirmed its order of November 12 on the basis of its review of the transcript of the evidentiary hearing of November 11. In this addendum, the appeals board noted that the JI had failed to present adequate evidence to support their case.

After limited hearings on the slurry wall construction, the ASLB issued its decision authorizing NIPSCO to proceed as planned with the slurry wall, on the condition that NIPSCO pursue two actions designed to protect the environment. First, if the slurry wall failed to work as planned, the board required NIPSCO to notify the AEC before implementing any alternative means to prevent dewatering of the dunes. Second, the AEC directed its staff to assure that NIPSCO complied with the first condition (LPB-74-85).

The JI followed up on this decision with an appeal to the ASLAB to reopen the hearings on construction of the slurry wall, protesting the short length of time made available to develop their case in the earlier hearing.

A farrago of oral and written motions, petitions, and demands there-upon descended upon the licensing board. In a very brief period of time that board was asked, among other things, to convene the hearing at the earliest possible date; to delay the hearing until after the Court of Appeals argument; to permit Illinois to intervene; to exclude Illinois from the proceeding; to disqualify a board member; to allow extra time to file prepared testimony; to order additional discovery; and to postpone the hearing schedule. The board dealt with those and other problems with dispatch.[17]

The ASLAB further noted that while the slurry wall itself was a proven technology, the specific methods of construction that NIPSCO pro-posed had never been tested in the United States. The appeals board there-fore agreed with the JI that a reopening of hearings on the slurry wall was necessary. However, the board specified that the hearings be limited to cross-examination of witnesses who had appeared at the previous hearing and to presentation of an affirmative case on the JI's behalf. The board specifically prohibited further discovery procedures. The rehearing would be before the ASLB (ALAB-249).

The ASLB presented its findings from the rehearing on February 21, 1975, determining that "the potential environmental benefit from slurry wall construction substantially outweighs the negligible adverse impacts associated with the slurry wall proposal."[18] The board's decision was, in part, based on a revised cost-benefit analysis including the cost of the wall. Again,

---

17 Ibid.
18 NRC, *Issuances*, 1976, p. 983.

the ASLB approved the slurry wall, reiterating the conditions it had spelled out in its decision of November 22, 1974.

At this point the JI pursued their case outside the NRC administrative system, in the U.S. Federal Circuit Court, Seventh Circuit, charging that the NRC had violated its own regulations in authorizing NIPSCO's permit to build the Bailly facility. JI argued that the NRC should have calculated the distance from the Bailly site to the nearest population center from the border of that center (the city of Porter) rather than from the central part of the city. (This challenge is reminiscent of Hansis's "rubber yardstick," and the "deduced" measurements of the utility, which the NRC supported.)

When the Court of Appeals found in favor of the JI in a case decided April 1, 1975 (515 F.2nd 513 [1975]), NIPSCO appealed the decision to the U.S. Supreme Court. Later that same year, the Supreme Court reversed the decision of the Appeals Court (423 US 12 [1975]), holding that the NRC, as the expert in the case, was responsible for establishing a methodology for calculating acceptable distance to population centers. The court remanded the case to the Appeals Court for a rehearing of the acceptable distance issue, along with additional charges that the JI had brought in its initial suit.

Among other challenges, the JI charged that the NRC lacked jurisdiction over the land on which the plant was sited. This land was immediately adjacent to the Indiana Dunes National Lakeshore, under control of the U.S. Department of the Interior. The Interior Department entered the controversy as a friend of the court, a role it pursued throughout the battle. In reality, Interior served the cause of the JI, drafting monthly reports documenting the impact of construction activity at the Bailly site on the nearby dunes with special attention to the concern about the dewatering at Cowles Bog.

In addition to these charges, the JI contended that the NRC had failed to comply with the National Environmental Policy Act (NEPA) in the Bailly case. Furthermore, they charged that NIPSCO had failed to consider other sites and other sources of energy as alternatives to the Bailly nuclear facility, in spite of the fact that this information was included in the Environmental Impact Statement for the plant.

The Appeals Court found against the JI this time, while issuing a sympathetic decision that "does not imply any opinion concerning the merits of the agency's decision." Like the Supreme Court, the Appeals Court deferred to the expertise of the NRC and based its decision on procedural, rather than substantive considerations (533 F.2nd 1011 [1976]). The JI appealed this decision to the U.S. Supreme Court, which denied certiorari, thus ending appeals outside the NRC administrative system (429 US 945 [1976]).

NRC Reaffirms Slurry Wall Approval

Following this decision, the ASLAB reaffirmed the ASLB's approval of NIPSCO's request to build a slurry wall to prevent dewatering at the dunes. Furthermore, the ASLAB determined that the board had, in fact, "carried out in total measure its NEPA obligations with respect to the Bailly project in general and the concern for preserving the integrity of the National Lakeshore in particular (ALAB-303)."[19]

At this point, legal action by the JI subsided, but the battle was far from over.

Conflict of Interest

In May of 1977, the Joint Intervenors petitioned the NRC Board of Commissioners to review a decision of the director of NRC to deny their request to initiate proceedings to suspend NIPSCO's construction license for Bailly. The JI based their petition on their belief that the NRC staff had acted as an adversary on behalf of NIPSCO during the permit hearings. Invoking the Administrative Procedure Act, the JI charged the NRC with conflict of interest (CLI-78-7).

The NRC commissioners reviewed all previous decisions of the ASLB and the ASLAB and ruled that there had been no conflict of interest. The commissioners pointed to the fact that the decisions of the two NRC boards had been upheld in the U.S. federal court system, including the Supreme Court. They therefore refused to grant the JI's appeal.

Pilings

With this decision, the road to completion of the Bailly facility seemed smoothed. As construction activities seemed imminent, NIPSCO issued what it considered a clarification of its construction design, proposing to substitute shorter pilings for the original longer pilings in the foundation for the nuclear reactor (CLI-79-11).

The JI asked the NRC to reopen the construction permit hearings, arguing that the shorter pilings should be treated as an amendment to the initial design.

In rendering its decision, the commissioners distinguished between permits for construction and operation of nuclear facilities: "It is a fundamental precept of the Atomic Energy Act that possession of a construction permit is not a guarantee that the licensee will receive an operating license.

---

[19] Ibid., p. 876.

The licensee bears the risk that a plant which has received a construction permit may fail to pass muster at the operating license review stage."[20]

The commissioners pointed out that it was their opinion that the shorter pilings represented, as NIPSCO suggested, a clarification of a design element that the utility had intentionally left vague. They dismissed the JI's claim that the shorter pilings represented an actual design change from the original drawings. The commissioners further noted that NIPSCO, not the public, would have to bear the risk that if the shorter pilings proved inadequate, the ASLB would deny the utility an operating permit. They therefore refused to order hearings on the pilings issue. Instead, they charged the NRC staff with the responsibility to monitor the construction at Bailly, giving special attention to the adequacy of the shorter pilings. Furthermore, the commissioners authorized NRC staff to hold hearings or suspend construction if staff deemed it necessary.[21]

Permit Expiration

In the meantime, NIPSCO's time limit on its construction permit was running down. The utility began proceedings to extend its permit deadline. The Joint Intervenors joined the fray, requesting standing to participate in the hearings on the extension (LBP-80-22).

NIPSCO's construction permit required that the utility complete construction of the Bailly facility by September 1, 1979, the expiration date of the permit. The NRC was authorized to extend the deadline, but only if the utility could show that its failure to meet the deadline was caused by factors beyond its control. NIPSCO requested an extension until December 1, 1987.

The licensing board refused to grant standing to the JI, and the appeals board reaffirmed that decision, noting that "a permit extension proceeding is not convened for the purpose of conducting an open-ended inquiry into the safety and environmental aspects of reactor construction and operation. Yet that is precisely what the proceeding would become were an open invitation given to those in petitioners' [JI's] situation to freight it unnecessarily with matters far removed from those events which led to its commencement" (ALAB-619).[22]

---

20 NRC, *Issuances*, 1980.

21 The commissioners raised but did not resolve the question of how the licensee should distribute the financial loss associated with a failed plant. This issue has so far fallen under the jurisdiction of state public utility commissions, not the NRC. While the issue is of compelling interest, it is outside the purview of this research.

22 NRC, *Issuances*, 1981, p. 573.

Pilings and Extensions

The ASLB held hearings on the construction permit extension in December. The Joint Intervenors sought to force NIPSCO to develop a new Environmental Impact Statement, an action that seemed to have been spurred by the accident at Three Mile Island (LBP-80-31). The board denied for litigation purposes the JI's contentions concerning the pilings issue and those unrelated to NIPSCO's proposed extension. Furthermore, the ASLB interpreted NEPA to require only a revised EIS in this case, rather than a completely new analysis. The JI once again attempted to force a hearing on the pilings issue as part of the permit extension request proceedings. The licensing board denied both requests.

The JI then asked the board to reconsider its ruling, or to refer the decision to the appeals board or to the NRC Board of Commissioners. The ASLB denied this request as well (LBP-81-6).

The End

NIPSCO continued to pursue its request for an extension until 1982, when the utility decided to abandon the Bailly plant, citing extraordinary cost escalation as the reason. The ASLB approved NIPSCO's request for termination on the condition that the utility restore the Bailly site to its original condition (LBP-82-29).

The JI sought to have the project terminated with prejudice, a decision that would have foreclosed the possibility of NIPSCO's resurrecting the Bailly plant at a later date. The board ruled that, since there had been no decision adverse to the Bailly facility, a termination without prejudice was the appropriate action.

NIPSCO's request for an extension thus was allowed to expire along with its original permit. The NRC ordered the utility to restore the site forthwith.

The ASLB issued the final order terminating the Bailly facility on May 6, 1982. In so doing, the board ordered NRC staff to supervise closely NIPSCO's restoration activities, as had been suggested by the JI (LBP-82-37).

In spite of the fact that it lost most of the battles in this long war of attrition, in the end, the JI won the war. They had stopped Bailly, largely as a result of their delay tactics and in spite of the consistent reaffirmation of the Bailly site by the NRC.

The Bailly case provides fine examples of many of the ideas discussed in earlier chapters. Most notably, the shift of the Bailly controversy from the administrative courts of the NRC to the federal court system illustrates the deference of the legal system to the technical expertise of the NRC. It is evident that the NRC exercised considerable discretion over the fate of NIPSCO's proposed nuclear facility at the Bailly site. Ultimately, however, economic factors beyond the control of all the actors were the deciding issues.

The next chapter, which opens Part 3, provides an analysis of the NRC's decisions in the Bailly case, focusing on the relationship between the NRC and its client groups.

Chapter 7

ANALYSIS

In identifying empirical evidence of influence in the NRC's decisions in the Bailly case, my analytical approach is twofold, identifying incidents that suggest that there is influence, and taking an overview approach, looking at the decisions as a trend.

The purpose of this dual approach is to address the limitations of the adversarial nature of the process. The adversarial nature of the Nuclear Regulatory Commission's role in nuclear siting decisions has implications for the way the agency carries out its responsibilities and ultimately, for the outcomes. The NRC is brought into the siting decision after the utility has made its initial choice of a location for the facility. The utility must justify its choice of a site in its Environmental Impact Statement and satisfy NRC requirements that the site chosen conforms to agency standards, such as minimum distance from population centers. Implicit in this arrangement is the notion that unless there is opposition, the utility and the NRC have a limited basis for disagreement. Once the NRC has approved construction of a specific facility at a specific site, as it did with Bailly, it has fulfilled its basic regulatory responsibility. While the agency is responsible for continued routine monitoring of the activities, if there is no opposition, its next decision comes when the utility applies for an operating license. Thus the regulatory process is spurred, if not fueled, by organized opposition.

In the Bailly case, the Joint Intervenors supplied the organized opposition. Each time the JI entered the regulatory process by challenging some aspect of the Bailly facility or proceedings, they risked a negative decision. Therefore, an examination of raw numbers and percentages has limited usefulness as a tool for identifying influence or describing the significance of the organization-client relationship in the Bailly case. It is useful as a starting point, however.

Historical Context

The Bailly case must be viewed in its proper historical context. The decade of the 1970s stands as one of the most significant decades in the history of energy. Two major incidents—the Arab oil embargo of 1973 and the nuclear accident at Three Mile Island in 1979—had profound influences on energy and on the public's perception of energy in the United States.

The Arab oil embargo had a two-stage impact on U.S. energy. The initial response to the embargo was to emphasize alternatives to foreign oil wherever possible. While converting automobiles to nonpetroleum fuels was virtually impossible for both technical and economic reasons, electrical generating facilities offered greater potential for alternative fuels.

The Bailly plant was licensed in 1972. With the advent of the oil embargo a year later, NIPSCO's timing seemed perfect. With energy demand predicted to increase, and the utility set to build a generating facility fueled by a source independent of Middle East politics, the construction of Bailly would seem to have been a foregone conclusion. Had the utility chosen another, less controversial site, away from the tightly knit, readily mobilized residents of Dune Acres, it may indeed have succeeded in building its plant. It is difficult to do other than to speculate about a path not chosen, however.

The second-phase response to the embargo, conservation, was partly to blame for the the demise of the Bailly facility. Spurred by the higher prices precipitated by the embargo and the resulting decreased supply of petroleum, as well as by policies established during the Carter administration, U.S. citizens began to seek ways to conserve energy of all kinds. Less driving, thermostats set lower in winter and higher in summer, and weatherization were all part of the picture. By the end of the 1970s, earlier estimates of energy demand in the United States were revised downward to account for the success of conservation efforts.

Furthermore, a decline in the fortunes of the steel and refinery industries in the United States in the late seventies contributed to the downwardly revised estimates of energy demand for NIPSCO's industrial customers. A region dependent on steel and refineries, northwestern Indiana was hit hard as industry's needs for energy declined along with employment, profits, and other trappings of successful industry.

The nuclear accident at Three Mile Island (TMI) struck a deadly blow to the Bailly facility. Semple and Richetto were prophetic when they discussed phase three of the nuclear energy product cycle.[1] After a period of ex-

---

[1]   R.K. Semple and J.P. Richetto, "Locational Trends of an Experimental Public Facility: The Case of Nuclear Power Plants," *Professional Geographer*, v. 28, n. 3, (August 1976): 248-53.

pansion in the early 1970s, the entire nuclear industry—not just Bailly—
was brought to its knees by TMI. Public sentiment, which previously had
either embraced nuclear energy as a viable alternative to foreign oil or expressed indifference, now rejected nuclear energy as a dangerous, imperfectly tested technology.

Evidence of Influence

At first glance, the overall picture presented by the numerous decisions of the NRC in the Bailly case suggests that the Joint Intervenors were
on the short end of the decision stick. Such an assessment, however, is too
facile. A closer look suggests that the JI came off somewhat better than that.
The very fact that they were granted standing to challenge NIPSCO is itself a
victory of sorts. In fact, one reason that the list of intervenors is so long is
that BPI warned the Concerned Citizens that their request for standing
might fail, and counselled them to improve their chances that one of their
number win standing simply by increasing their numbers. James Newman
of the Concerned Citizens recounted his surprise that all who sued for
standing were granted their request.[2]

In addition to standing, the NRC granted the JI multiple extensions
in 1972 to enable them to prepare their arguments. This suggests that the
agency attempted to deal with its clients evenhandedly. In fact, in one case,
the NRC granted an extension in exasperation—but granted it nonetheless.

It should be noted that the JI went before the administrative boards of
the AEC/NRC charging those very boards with bias. Lest we forget, real
people work at the NRC. That the agency apparently attempted to operate
"without regard for persons" is to its credit.

Still, the decisions of the NRC favored NIPSCO far more frequently
than they favored the JI. Actual won/lost percentages at first glance indicate
that the NRC did indeed show signs of bias in its decisions. During the
course of the Bailly conflict, NIPSCO solicited a decision from the agency
three times, winning two of those decisions (66%). The JI went before the
NRC twenty-two times, also winning just two of those decisions (9.1%).

It seems to have made virtually no difference from which tier of the
NRC administrative courts the JI sought relief. They went before the
Atomic Safety and Licensing Board (ASLB) five times, winning once (20%).
They sought relief from the Atomic Safety and Licensing Appeals Board
(ASLAB) thirteen times, winning once (about 8%), losing ten times (about
77%), and getting two split decisions (about 15%). Out of four times before
the full Nuclear Regulatory Commission, the JI won once (25%).

---

2   James Newman, interview with author at Indiana University Northwest, Gary Ind.,
March 1985.

NIPSCO, on the other hand, won both times it went before the ASLB (100%). It lost, however, on the only occasion when it sought relief from the ASLAB. Overall, the evidence suggests that the NRC tended to favor NIPSCO in its decisions. The degree to which this is the case, however, is open to question. While the raw numbers strongly suggest bias, there is the argument that a request for a decision gives the agency an opportunity to rule—either favorably or unfavorably—on the request.

When we consider the evidence suggesting that the Bailly site was objectionable on both safety and environmental counts, we are faced with a gnawing problem: each time the question of the appropriateness of the Bailly site was challenged, the NRC reaffirmed the site. The U.S. Supreme Court declined to rule on the substantive criteria the regulator used to justify the choice of site, and restricted the Court of Appeals to a purely administrative (procedural) review as well. Under the circumstances, it is difficult to maintain that the NRC made its decisions free of influence.

If the JI failed to exercise influence equal to that of the utility in actual decisions, they were very successful in gaining access to the decision-making process in the first instance. As a strategic move, access to the system is perhaps the next best thing to a favorable decision. According to James Newman, an important part of the group's strategy was to stall construction, hoping eventually to kill the project through attrition if not by outright decision.[3] In this case, access to administrative decision-makers is a crucial tool. From this perspective, the grant of standing is a major victory, which the JI were able to parlay into twenty-two subsequent challenges of the Bailly siting decision. Whether a war is won through attrition or by victory in one glorious battle may make little difference in the end.

Sources of Client Influence

Let us return, then, to the research question: how does the organization-client relationship affect locational decision-making? It is clear from its history as an organization that the AEC/NRC is caught between two client groups. The level of access to the process which the Joint Intervenors gained provides evidence that the agency did try to be fair. That so many decisions went against the JI suggests that in spite of its best efforts, the AEC/NRC was influenced by its desire to serve its client, NIPSCO.

The chronology of the AEC/NRC clearly points to a changing organizational mission. Initially, the agency's chief duty was to promote the use of nuclear energy. It would be wrong, however, to assume that the AEC's

---

[3]   Ibid.

mission changed overnight and that upon waking, it had magically become the NRC. In reality, the change was more gradual, an evolution rather than a revolution. Note, too, that the changed mission did not come from within the agency, but was mandated by Congress.

The evolution was already underway when the Bailly case began in 1972. By that time, the National Environmental Policy Act had already been passed, and President Nixon's executive order reiterated the national commitment to protect the environment.

On the other hand, the AEC had, since its inception, been in the business of promoting nuclear energy. The agency had worked with other utilities and, in fact, had probably dealt with the people at NIPSCO as well, as the utility prepared itself to seek a construction permit for Bailly. NIPSCO, therefore, for at least part of the Bailly conflict, enjoyed the benefits of both a historical and a legal relationship with the AEC. The AEC/NRC's relationship with the JI was initially based primarily on the requirements imposed upon the agency by NEPA, and later on President Nixon's executive order, and finally, on the transformation of the AEC into the NRC.

We might therefore expect to see an increase in victories by the JI following the reorganization of the AEC/NRC, when in fact, they suffered more defeats. Under both incarnations of the agency, NIPSCO won more decisions. It therefore appears that a historical relationship with an agency is probably more advantageous to a client than is a legally shared mission. This in turn suggests that the rule of capture applies in identification of clients.

Evidence from this case further suggests that the client with a stronger formal structure may have an edge in the organization-client relationship. In the Bailly case, the better-organized utility won more decisions than the JI, who claimed to speak on behalf of the public interest. This again points to the rule-of-capture argument.

However, we should not overlook the NRC's final decision on the Bailly case. In this decision, the agency agreed with the JI and ordered NIPSCO to return the Bailly site to its original condition. By this time, in the post–Three Mile Island era, public opinion had shifted to sympathy with the JI. NIPSCO had surrendered, and the NRC as an organization had little to lose by a decision in favor of the JI. On the other hand, the agency would have seemed very irresponsible, and risked damaging its credibility—and its legitimacy—had it not ordered the utility to restore the Bailly site. This suggests, then, that the regulatory agency will bow to public pressure when it can do so without seriously endangering its relationship with its client as defined by the rule of capture, and when succumbing to public pressure is necessary to renew its legitimacy.

The decisions on the Bailly case suggest, then, that an agency's locational decisions can be influenced by its clients. They further suggest that developing an enduring relationship with the organization takes time and a strong organizational commitment. Furthermore, the case suggests that a regulatory agency will tend to respond to a powerful, directed client over a dispersed clientele. However, if a generally dispersed clientele can organize as a coalition and frame its position as being in the public interest, then it may succeed in raising questions about the regulator's legitimacy. In order to restore its legitimacy, the regulator may feel the need to favor the public interest over the needs of its usual clients.

Chapter 8

CONCLUSIONS

The Bailly conflict is a web of interconnected client groups and responsive organizations. Of major concern in this paper was the relationship between the AEC/NRC and its dual clientele. At each level of decision and clients, we see further evidence of the organization responding to the needs of its clientele.

It is conceivable that the Bailly case might represent the early stages of an organizational learning curve. Consider the first twenty-five years of the Atomic Energy Commission/Nuclear Regulatory Agency. From its birth in 1947 until the reorganization of the agency in 1974, the AEC was a promoter of nuclear power. Under this interpretation, the regulator's postreorganization decisions reaffirming NIPSCO's choice of the Bailly site for its nuclear generating facility may reflect its short history as a nonpromoter of nuclear energy and a proponent of nuclear safety. In support of this position, the NRC's ordering NIPSCO to restore the Bailly site to its original condition stands as potential evidence of organizational learning.

However, this decision alone is insufficient to support an organizational learning curve hypothesis. Additional support of such a notion could come by way of NRC decisions on other facilities, or the agency's policy directions. The search for clear-cut evidence that the NRC has changed direction yields little.

While other once-planned nuclear generators have fallen by the wayside since Bailly, in general they owe their demise to the same factors that defeated Bailly: legal challenges, collective action, costly delays, and ultimately economic ruin—not the NRC—are the leading causes.

On the other hand, the NRC has voiced support for the development of a standard design for nuclear generating facilities in the United States. The idea behind this strategy is to eliminate some of the uncertainty about safety features of nuclear energy and thereby to decrease the risks involved with nuclear technology. This strategy is intended to address the legitimate safety concerns of the general public. From this perspective, it appears that the NRC is giving greater concern to its responsibility to the public interest.

Curiously, another policy direction that the NRC has pursued seems explicitly to ignore the public interest, that is, efforts by the agency to bypass the need for local evacuation plans, which currently are required before the NRC can grant an operating license. State and local governments have so far successfully blocked the granting of operating permits through their refusals to develop the required evacuation plans. If the NRC is successful in its efforts to win legislative backing for its position, state and local governments will lose an important weapon in their arsenals against nuclear facilities they believe are unsafe.

One is reminded of the NRC's response to the Joint Intervenors on the short pilings issue in the Bailly case. As you recall, the agency allowed the utility to substitute short pilings for longer pilings as a clarification of NIPSCO's original design. When the JI petitioned the NRC to require a new Environmental Impact Statement, the regulator, responding in favor of NIPSCO, cautioned that the utility would bear the risk that the NRC might deny an operating permit if the utility substituted short pilings. The NRC's current policy direction, which would decrease citizen input into the operating licensing, casts doubt on the agency's sincerity on the pilings issue. Indeed, the author's own experience in capital projects suggests that much informal discussion and even negotiation precedes formal requests for official action. My experience suggests that NIPSCO may very well have discussed the short pilings with the NRC and perhaps received unofficial assurances that the agency would not refuse to grant an operating permit.

On the basis of this evidence, I discount the notion that the NRC's decisions in the Bailly case merely represent the early stages of its learning curve in its new role as a regulator. A more compelling argument is that the NRC is responding to its clients, playing a balancing act, addressing the known needs of its traditional client, then as the agency's legitimacy comes into question, addressing the periodically vocalized public interest.

We should be aware of the impact of the political strength of clients. The Joint Intervenors are unique as a client group "on the outside." First, they were a highly sophisticated group, mostly well-educated, professional people. Just as important, they were a feisty group, cohesive on this single issue, and relatively well financed. In addition, they were able over the long run to capitalize on a changing public mood to raise questions about the NRC's legitimacy. For these reasons, they were able to wage—and win—a war of attrition against the Bailly plant.

Other client groups are not so fortunate. Many, perhaps most, lack cohesiveness and financial resources. The poor and the homeless are excellent examples of such disadvantaged client groups. While the system provides them access to the decision-making process, taking full advantage and making it work for the client requires resources: cohesiveness, time, energy, money, and more. Moreover, unless they can somehow raise the public consciousness and shift public interest to their cause (as was done in the 1960s in the case of civil rights, for example), they are unlikely to capture the target agency.

This book set out to answer the question of how the organization-client relationship affects locational decision-making. The Bailly case suggests that there is a link between organizations, clients, and decisions. In the case of the AEC/NRC, that link seemed to be stronger when it was backed by a historical relationship and a solid organizational structure with regard to the client.

This evidence suggests that it is important to consider the effects of state apparatus on geography. In the Bailly case, the bureaucratic structure of a state regulatory apparatus, coupled with limited judicial review of the activities of that apparatus, created a situation wherein the NRC repeatedly reaffirmed a site that was shown not to comply with the agency's own siting criteria. Had historical and economic events been different, the Bailly facility might well have been built.

It is apparent that the state matters, as many geographers have recognized. I have attempted to show that the structure of its apparatus matters as well.

In recent years, interest in citizen participation issues has grown, in a direction that may be especially fruitful when linked to organizational decision-making. It is my hope that this study can begin to open the door for such research.

BIBLIOGRAPHY

Adams, J.S. "A Geographical Basis for Urban Public Policy." *Professional Geographer*, v. 31, n. 2, February 1979.

Arnold, R.D. *Congress and the Bureaucracy: A Theory of Influence.* New Haven: Yale University Press, 1979.

Atomic Energy Commission. *Opinions and Decisions.* Washington, D.C.: U.S. Government Printing Office, 1970-74.

_____. *1972 Annual Report to Congress.* Washington, D.C.: U.S. Government Printing Office, 1973.Austin, M.; Smith, T.; and Wolpert, J. "The Implementation of Controversial Facility-Complex Programs." *Geographical Analysis*, v. 2, 1970.

Beard, D.P. "United States Environmental Legislation and Energy Resources: A Review." *Geographical Review*, v. 65, n. 2, April 1975.

Bennett, R.J. *The Geography of Public Finance.* London: Methuen, 1980.

Berry, B.J.L. "On Geography and Urban Policy." In *Urban Policymaking and Metropolitan Dynamics: A Comparative Geographical Analysis,* edited by John S. Adams. Cambridge, Mass.: Ballinger, 1976.

Bohland, J.R., and Gist, J. "The Spatial Consequences of Bureaucratic Decision-Making." *Environment and Planning-A,* v. 15, n. 11, November 1983.

Brubaker, Rogers. *The Limits of Rationality.* Boston: George Allen and Unwin, 1984.

Brunn, S.D., and Hoffman, W.L. "The Geography of Federal Grants-in-Aid to States." *Economic Geography,* v. 45, n. 6, 1969.

Burnett, A.D., and Taylor, P.J., eds. *Political Studies from Spatial Perspectives.* New York: John Wiley and Sons, 1981.

Burns, E.K. "Financial Analysis of Suburban Annexation Alternatives." *Professional Geographer,* v. 33, n. 2, February 1981.

Business and Professional People for the Public Interest (BPI). "Aftermath of Bailly Victory: Utility Agrees to Restore Site and Fill in Excavation." *BPI Newsletter*, Winter 1981.

Caldwell, L.K. *Man and His Environment: Policy and Administration* New York: Harper and Row, 1975.

Caldwell, L.K., and MacWhirter, I.M. *Citizens and the Environment: Case Studies in Popular Action.* Bloomington: Indiana University Press, 1976.

Campbell, A.K. "Old and New Public Administration in the 1970s." *Public Administration Review*, v. 32, n. 4, July-August 1972.

Christensen, K. *Social Impacts of Land Development.* Washington, D.C.: Urban Land Institute, 1976.

Civiak, R. *Nuclear Regulatory Commission Organizational History.* Congressional Research Service. Washington, D.C.: U.S. Government Printing Office, 1982.

Clark, G.L. "Urban Impact Analysis: A New Tool for Monitoring the Geographical Effects of Federal Policies." *Professional Geographer*, v. 32, n. 1, January 1980.

_____. "Law, the State and the Spatial Integration of the United States." *Environment and Planning-A*, v. 13, n. 10, October 1981.

_____. Review of *The Geography of Public Finance*, by R.J. Bennett. In *Progress in Human Geography*, v. 6, n. 4, 1983.

_____. Review of *Geography and the State*, by R.J. Johnston. In *Environment and Planning D: Society and Space*, v. 1, n. 4, 1983.

_____. *Judges and the Cities.* Chicago: University of Chicago Press, 1985.

Clark, G.L., and Dear, M.J. *State Apparatus.* Boston: Allen and Unwin, 1984.

Clark, G.L., and Gertler, M. "Local Labor Markets: Theories and Policies in the United States during the 1970s." *Professional Geographer*, v. 35, n. 3, August 1983.

Clarke, M., and Prentice, R. "Exploring Decisions in Public Policy-Making: Strategic Allocation, Individual Allocation and Simulation." *Environment and Planning-A*, v. 14, n. 3, 1982.

Cleary, P. "Nuclear Power: The Risks to Lake Michigan." *Lake Michigan Papers Series.* Chicago: Lake Michigan Federation, 1979.

Commoner, B. *The Poverty of Power.* New York: Bantam, 1977.

_____. *The Politics of Energy.* New York: Alfred A. Knopf, 1979.

Cutter, S., and Barnes, K. "Evacuation Behavior and Three Mile Island." *Disasters*, v. 6, 1982.

Dear, M.J. "A Paradigm for Public Facility Location Theory." *Antipode*, v. 6, n. 1, April 1974.

_____. "Locational Factors in the Demand for Mental Health Care." *Economic Geography*, v. 53, n. 3, March 1977.

_____. "The State: A Research Agenda." *Environment and Planning-A*, v. 13, n. 10, October 1981.

_____. Review of *Geography and the State*, by R.J. Johnston. *Environment and Planning-A*, v. 15, n. 10, October 1983.

Dear, M.J., and Clark, G.L. "Dimensions of Local State Autonomy." *Environment and Planning-A*, v. 13, n. 10, October 1981.

Dear, M.J., and Clark, G.L. "The State and Geographic Process: A Critical Review." *Environment and Planning-A*, v. 10, n. 2, February 1978.

Dear, M.J., and Taylor, M. *Not on Our Street: Community Attitudes toward Mental Health Care*. London: Pion, 1982.

Dear, M.J.; Taylor, M.; and Hall, G.B. "External Effects of Mental Health Facilities." *Annals of the Association of American Geographers*, v. 70, n. 3, 1980.

Dikshit, R.D. "Geography and Federalism." *Annals of the Association of American Geographers,*, v. 61, n. 1, January-February 1971.

Diver, C.S. "Policymaking Paradigms in Administrative Law." *Harvard Law Review*, v. 95, n. 2, December 1981.

Downs, Anthony. *Inside Bureaucracy*. Boston: Little, Brown and Co., 1966.

Drucker, P. *Management: Tasks, Responsibilities and Practices*. New York: Harper and Row, 1974.

_____. *Managing in Turbulent Times*. New York: Harper and Row, 1980.

Engel, J.R. *Sacred Sands: The Struggle for Community at the Indiana Dunes*. Middletown, Conn.: Wesleyan University Press, 1983.

Eyles, J.; Smith, D.M.; and Woods, K.J. "Spatial Resource Allocation and State Practice: The Case of Health Service Planning in London." *Regional Studies*, v. 16, n. 4, 1982.

Fesler, James N. "Public Administration and the Social Sciences: 1946-60." In *American Public Administration: Past, Present, Future*, edited by F.C. Mosher. University: University of Alabama Press, 1976.

Fincher, R. "Local Implementation Strategies in the Urban Built Environment." *Environment and Planning-A*, v. 13, n. 10, October 1981.

Finer, Herman. "Administrative Responsibility in Democratic Government." In *Bureaucratic Power in National Politics*, edited by Francis E. Rourke. Boston: Little, Brown and Co., 1978.

Flowerdew, R., ed. *Institutions and Geographical Patterns*. New York: St. Martin's Press, 1982.

Flowerdew, R., and Manion, T. Introduction to *Institutions and Geographical Patterns*, edited by R. Flowerdew, pp. 1-50. New York: St. Martin's Press, 1982.

Forester, J. "The Geography of Planning Practice." *Environment and Planning D: Society and Space*, v. 2, n. 3, 1983.

_____, ed. *Critical Theory and Public Life*. Cambridge, Mass.: Massachusetts Institute of Technology Press, 1985.

Friedrich, Carl J. "Public Policy and the Nature of Administrative Responsibility." In *Bureaucratic Power in National Politics*, edited by Francis E. Rourke. Boston: Little, Brown and Co., 1978.

Fuchs, R., and Demko, G. "Geographic Inequality under Socialism." *Annals of the Association of American Geographers*, v. 69, n. 2, June 1979.

Gerth, H.H., and Mills, C. Wright. *From Max Weber: Essays in Sociology*. New York: Oxford University Press, 1946.

Gibson, Frank, "Organizations and Their Environments: The School System as a Focus." In *Public Administration: Readings in Institutions, Processes, Behavior, Policy*, edited by R.T. Golembiewski, F. Gibson, and G.Y. Cornog. Chicago: Rand McNally College Publishing Co., 1976.

Golembiewski, R.T.; Gibson, F.; and Cornog, G.Y., eds. *Public Administration: Readings in Institutions, Processes, Behavior, Policy*. Chicago: Rand McNally College Publishing Co., 1976.

Goodsell, C.T. *The Case for Bureaucracy: A Public Administration Polemic*. Chatham, N.J.: Chatham House Publishers, 1985.

Gould, S.J. *Ontogeny and Phylogeny*. Cambridge, Mass.: The Belknap Press of Harvard University Press, 1977.

_____. *The Mismeasure of Man*. New York: W.W. Norton and Co.,1981.

Green, D.G. "The Spatial Sciences and the State." *Environment and Planning-A*, v. 14, n. 11, November 1982.

Grodzins, Morton, "The Many American Governments and Outdoor Recreation." In *Public Administration: Readings in Institutions, Processes, Behavior, Policy*, edited by R.T. Golembiewski, F. Gibson, and G.Y. Cornog. Chicago: Rand McNally College Publishing Co., 1976.

Habermas, Jurgen. *Toward a Rational Society: Student Protest, Science, and Politics*. Translated by Jeremy J. Shapiro. Boston: Beacon Press, 1970.

_____. *The Theory of Communicative Action. Vol. 1, Reason and the Rationalization of Society*. Translated by Thomas McCarthy. Boston: Beacon Press, 1981.

Hall, P. *Great Planning Disasters*. Berkeley: University of California Press, 1981.

Hansis, R. "Emergency Planning and Nuclear Power Plant Siting in Northwest Indiana." Paper presented at the Annual Meeting of the Association of American Geographers, Louisville, Ky., in April 1980.

Harmon, Michael M. "Administrative Policy Formulations." In *Public Administration Readings in Institutions, Processes, Behavior, Policy*, edited by R.T. Golembiewski, F. Gibson, and G.Y. Cornog. Chicago: Rand McNally College Publishing Co., 1976.

Haynes, K.E.; Phillips, F.Y.; and Solomon, B.D. "A Coal Industry Distribution Planning Model under Environmental Constraints." *Economic Geography*, v. 59, n. 1, January 1983.

Hodgart, R.L. "Optimizing Access to Public Services: A Review of Problems, Models, and Methods of Locating Central Facilities." *Progress in Human Geography*, 1978, n. 2.

Hodge, D., and Gatrell, A. "Spatial Constraints and the Location of Urban Public Facilities." *Environment and Planning-A*, 1976.

Hodgson, M.J. "Toward a More Realistic Allocation in Location-Allocation Models: An Interaction Approach." *Environment and Planning-A*, 1978, v. 10.

Hoggart, K. "Social Needs, Political Representation, and Federal Outlays in the East North Central United States of America." *Environment and Planning-A*, v. 13, n. 5, May 1981.

Holden, Matthew, Jr. "Imperialism in Bureaucracy." In *Bureaucratic Power in National Politics*, edited by Francis E. Rourke. Boston: Little, Brown and Co., 1978.

Johnson, J.H., Jr., and Zeigler, D. "Distinguishing Human Response to Radiological Emergencies." *Economic Geography*, v. 59 (1983).

Johnston, R.J. "The Management and Autonomy of the Local State: The Role of the Judiciary in the U.S." *Environment and Planning-A*, v. 13, n. 10, October 1981.

_____.*Geography and the State*. New York: St. Martin's Press, 1982.

Jones, K., and Kirby, A. "Provision and Well-Being: An Agenda for Public Resources Research." *Environment and Planning-A*, v. 14, n. 3, 1982.

Kaufman, H. *Time, Chance and Organizations: Natural Selection in a Perilous Environment*. Chatham, N.J.: Chatham House Publishers, 1985.

Kednay, L.B. "Environmental Politics at the Indiana Dunes." Typescript, 1977.

Keyes, D.L. *Land Development and the Natural Environment: Estimating Impacts*. Washington, D.C.: Urban Institute, 1976.

Komaiko, J., and Schaeffer, N. *Doing the Dunes.* Beverly Shores, Ind.: Dunes Enterprises, 1973.

Lindal, E. "Just Taxation—a positive solution." In *Classics in the Economics of Public Finance,* edited by R. Musgrave and J. Peacock. London: Macmillan, 1958.

Long, Norton E. "Power and Administration." In *Bureaucratic Power in National Politics,* edited by Francis E. Rourke. Boston: Little, Brown and Co., 1978.

Lorch, R.S. *Democratic Process and Administrative Law.* Detroit: Wayne State University Press, 1969.

Lowi, T.J. *The End of Liberalism.* New York: W.W. Norton and Co., 1969.

McAllister, D.M. "Equity and Efficiency in Public Facility Location." *Geographical Analysis,* v. 8, 1976.

McNee, R.N. "Regional Planning, Bureaucracy, and Geography." *Economic Geography,* v. 46, n. 2, April 1970.

March, J.G., and Olsen, J.P. "The New Institutionalism: Organizational Factors in Political Life." *American Political Science Review,* v. 78, 1984.

March, James G., and Simon, Herbert A. *Organizations.* New York: John Wiley and Sons, 1958.

Massam, B. *Location and Space in Social Administration.* New York: John Wiley and Sons, 1975.

Mayer, H.M. "Politics and Land Use: The Indiana Shoreline of Lake Michigan." *Annals of the Association of American Geographers,* v. 54 December 1964,.

Mercer, D. "Conflict over a High Voltage Power Line: A Victoria Case Study." *Australian Geographer,* v. 15, n. 5, May 1983.

Mercer, J., and Hultquist, J. "National Progress Toward Housing and Urban Renewal Goals." In *Urban Policymaking and Metropolitan Dynamics: A Comparative Geographical Analysis,* edited by J.S. Adams. Cambridge, Mass.: Ballinger, 1976.

Merton, R.K.; Gray, A.P.; Hockey, B.; and Selvin, H.C., eds. *Reader in Bureaucracy.* New York: Free Press, 1952.

Moore, C.L. "The Impact of Public Institutions on Regional Income, Upstate Medical Center as a Case in Point." *Economic Geography,* v. 50, n. 2, April 1974.

Morrill, R.L. "Efficiency and Equity of Optimum Location Models." *Antipode,* v. 6, 1974.

Mosher, F.C., ed. *American Public Administration: Past, Present, Future.* University, Ala.: University of Alabama Press, 1976.

Moss, E., ed. *Land Use Controls in the United States.* New York: Dial Press, 1977.

Mouzelis, James. *Organisation and Bureaucracy: An Analysis of Modern Theories* Chicago: Aldine Publishing Co., 1967.

Muller, T. *Economic Impacts of Land Development.* Washington, D.C.: Urban Institute, 1976.

Mumphrey, A.J., and Wolpert, J. "Equity Considerations and Concessions in the Siting of Public Facilities." *Economic Geography,* v. 94, 1973.

Nash, R., ed. *The American Environment: Readings in the History of Conservation.* Reading, Mass.: Addison-Wesley, 1968.

Newman, J. Introduction to untitled manuscript on the Bailly controversy.

Nuclear Regulatory Commission. *Issuances: Opinions and Decisions of the Nuclear Regulatory Commission with Selected Orders.* Washington, D.C.: U.S. Government Printing Office, 1974-83.

Osleeb, J.P. "An Evaluation of the Strategic Petroleum Reserve Program of the U.S. Department of Energy." *Professional Geographer,* v. 31, n. 4, November 1979.

Papageorgiou, G.J. "Spatial Externalities: Parts I and II." *Annals of the Association of American Geographers,* v. 68, 1978.

Peters, B.G. *The Politics of Bureaucracy.* New York: Longman, 1984.

Pijawka, D., and Chalmers, J. "Impacts of Nuclear Generating Plants on Local Areas." *Economic Geography,* v. 59, n. 1, January 1983.

Platt, R.H. *The Open Space Decision Process.* University of Chicago Department of Geography Research Papers, no. 142. Chicago: University of Chicago Department of Geography, 1972.

Pressman, J.L., and Wildavsky, A.B. *Implementation: How Great Expectations in Washington are Dashed in Oakland; or, Why It's Amazing that Federal Programs Work at All.* Berkeley: University of California Press, 1973.

Pugh, D.S., ed. *Organization Theory.* Baltimore: Penguin Books, 1973.

Redman, E. *The Dance of Legislation.* New York: Simon and Schuster, 1973.

ReVelle, C.S., and Swain, R.W. "Central Facilities Location." *Geographical Analysis,* v. 2, 1970.

Robbins, R.L. "The Lake Michigan Manifesto: A Statement of New Principles for Directing How We Use Lake Michigan and a Program to Carry out Those Principles." *Lake Michigan Papers Series* Chicago: Lake Michigan Federation, 1981.

Rojeski, P., and ReVelle, C.S. "Central Facilities Location under an Investment Constraint." *Geographical Analysis,* v. 2, 1970.

Rosenbaum, W.A. *The Politics of Environmental Concern.* New York: Praeger Publishers, 1974.

Ross, R.J.S. "Facing Leviathan: Public Policy and Global Capitalism." *Economic Geography,* v. 59, n. 2, April 1983.

Rourke, Francis E. "Variations in Agency Power." In *Bureaucratic Power in National Politics,* edited by Francis E. Rourke. Boston: Little, Brown and Co., 1978.

_____, ed. *Bureaucratic Power in National Politics* Boston: Little, Brown and Co., 1978.

Rowe, P.G.; Mixon, J.; Smith, B.A.; Blackburn, J.B., Jr.; Callaway, G.L.; and Gevirtz, J.L. *Principles for Local Environmental Management.* Cambridge, Mass.: Ballinger Publishing Co., 1978.

Roweis, Shoukry. "Urban Planning in Early and Late Capitalist Society: Outline of a Theoretical Perspective." In *Urbanization and Urban Planning in Capitalist Society,* edited by Dear and Scott. New York: Methuen, 1981.

_____. "Urban Planning as Professional Mediation of Territorial Politics," *Environment and Planning D: Society and Space,* n. 1, 1982.

Samuelson, P.A. "The Pure Theory of Public Expenditures." *Review of Economics and Statistics,* v. 36, 1954, pp. 387-89.

Schaenman, P.S. *Using and Impact Measurement System to Evaluate Land Development.* Washington, D.C.: Urban Institute, 1976.

Schaenman, P.S., and Muller, T. *Measuring Impacts of Land Development.* Washington, D.C.: Urban Institute, 1976.

Schick, Allen, "The Trauma of Politics: Public Administration in the Sixties." In *American Public Administration: Past, Present, and Future,* edited by Frederick C. Mosher. University: University of Alabama Press, 1976.

Schwartz, B. *Administrative Law.* Boston: Little, Brown and Co., 1976.

Semple, R.K., and Richetto, J.P. "Locational Trends of an Experimental Public Facility: The Case of Nuclear Power Plants." *Professional Geographer,* v. 28, n. 3, August 1976.

Shapiro, P., and Smith, T.R. "Public Policy Assessment: Evaluating Objectives of Resource Policies." *Economic Geography,* v. 55, n. 2, April 1979.

Simon, Herbert A. *Administrative Behavior.* New York: Free Press, 1945.

Simon, Herbert A.; Smithburg, Donald W.; and Thompson, Victor A. "The Struggle for Organizational Survival." In *Bureaucratic Power in National Politics,* edited by Francis E. Rourke. Boston: Little, Brown and Co., 1978.

Smit, B., and Johnston, R.J. "Public Policy Assessment: Evaluating Objectives of Resource Policies." *Professional Geographer*, v. 35, n. 2, February 1983.

Starling, G. *Managing the Public Sector*. Homewood, Ill.: Dorsey Press, 1977.

Stewart, R.B. "The Discontents of Legalism: Interest Group Relations in Administrative Regulation." *Wisconsin Law Review*, v. 1985, n. 3.

_____. "Reconstitutive Law." presented as the Simon E. Sobeloff Lecture at the University of Maryland Law School in April 1985.

Storper, M.; Walker, R.; and Widess, B. "Performance Regulation and Industrial Location: A Case Study." *Environment and Planning-A*, v. 13, n. 3, March 1981.

Taylor, P.W. *Respect for Nature: A Theory of Environmental Ethics* Princeton, N.J.: Princeton University Press, 1986.

Teitz, M.B. "Toward a Theory of Urban Public Facility Location." *Papers, Regional Science Association*, v. 21, 1968 Cambridge meeting, November 1967,.

Thompson, James D. *Organizations in Action*. New York: McGraw-Hill Book Co., 1967.

Thompson, Victor A. *Bureaucracy and the Modern World*. Morristown, N.J.: General Learning Press, 1976.

Thrall, G.I. "Public Goods and the Derivation of Land Value Assessment Schedule within a Spatial Equilibrium Setting." *Geographical Analysis*, v. 11, n. 1, January 1979.

_____. "Spatial Inequities in Tax Assessment: A Case Study of Hamilton, Ontario." *Economic Geography*, v. 55, n. 2, April 1979.

_____. "Dynamics in the Structural Form of Property Taxes." *Professional Geographer*, v. 33, n. 4, April 1981.

Thrall, G.I., and Casetti, E. "Local Public Goods and Spatial Equilibrium in an Ideal Urban Center." *Canadian Geographer*, v. 22, Winter 1978.

Tiebout, C.M. "A Pure Theory of Local Expenditures." *Journal of Political Economy*, v. 64, n. 5, 1956.

Tomain, J.P., and Hollis, S.S. *Energy Decision Making*. Lexington, Mass.: Lexington Books, 1983.

Wagner, J.L., and Falkson, L.M. "The Optimal Nodal Location of Public Facilities with Price-Sensitive Demand." *Geographical Analysis*, v. 7, 1975.

Weber, Max. *The Protestant Ethic and the Spirit of Capitalism*. Translated by Talcott Parsons. New York: Scribner's, 1958.

Weber, Max. *Economy and Society*. Ed. Guenther Roth and Claus Wittich. Berkeley: University of California Press, 1968.

Whiteman, J. "Deconstructing the Tiebout Hypothesis." *Environment and Planning D: Society and Space*, v. 1, n. 3, 1983.

Wildavsky, A. *The Politics of the Budgetary Process*. Boston: Little, Brown and Co., 1974.

Willbern, Y. "Types and Levels of Public Morality." *Public Administration Review*, v. 44, n. 2, March-April 1984.

Williams, P. "Restructuring Urban Managerialism: Towards a Political Economy of Urban Allocation." *Environment and Planning-A*, v. 14, n. 1, January 1982.

Wilson, James Q. "The Rise of the Bureaucratic State." In *Bureaucratic Power in National Politics*, edited by Francis E. Rourke. Boston: Little, Brown and Co., 1978.

Wohlenberg, E.H. "Public Assistance Effectiveness by States." *Annals of the Association of American Geographers*, v. 66, n. 3, 1976.

_____. "Interstate Variations in AFDC Programs." *Economic Geography*, v. 52, n. 3, 1979.

Wolch, J.R., and Gabriel, S.A. "Local Land Development Policies and Urban Housing Values." *Environment and Planning-A*, v. 13, n. 10, October 1981.

Yellin, J. "High Technology and the Courts: Nuclear Power and the Need for Institutional Reform." *Harvard Law Review*, v. 94, n. 3, January 1981.

Zeigler, D.; Brunn, S.D.; and Johnson, J.H., Jr. "Evacuation from a Nuclear Technological Disaster." *Geographical Review*, v. 71, 1981.

Zeigler, D., and Johnson, J.H., Jr. "Evacuation Behavior in Response to Nuclear Power Plant Accidents." *Professional Geographer*, v. 36, n. 2, 1984.

Index

THE UNIVERSITY OF CHICAGO
GEOGRAPHY RESEARCH PAPERS
(Lithographed, 6 x 9 inches)

Titles in Print

121. BAUMANN, DUANE D. *The Recreational Use of Domestic Water Supply Reservoirs: Perception and Choice*. 1969. ix + 125 p.

122. LIND, AULIS O. *Coastal Landforms of Cat Island, Bahamas: A Study of Holocene Accretionary Topography and Sea-Level Change*. 1969. ix + 156 p.

123. WHITNEY, JOSEPH B. R. *China: Area, Administration and Nation Building*. 1970. xiii + 198 p.

124. EARICKSON, ROBERT. *The Spatial Behavior of Hospital Patients: A Behavioral Approach to Spatial Interaction in Metropolitan Chicago*. 1970. xi + 138 p.

125. DAY, JOHN C. *Managing the Lower Rio Grande: An Experience in International River Development*. 1970. xii + 274 p.

126. MacIVER, IAN. *Urban Water Supply Alternatives: Perception and Choice in the Grand Basin, Ontario*. 1970. ix + 178 p.

127. GOHEEN, PETER G. *Victorian Toronto, 1850 to 1900: Pattern and Process of Growth*. 1970. xiii + 278 p.

128. GOOD, CHARLES M.*Rural Markets and Trade in East Africa*. 1970. xvi + 252 p.

129. MEYER, DAVID R. *Spatial Variation of Black Urban Households*. 1970. xiv + 127 p.

130. GLADFELTER, BRUCE G. *Meseta and Campina Landforms in Central Spain: A Geomorphology of the Alto Henares Basin*. 1971. xii + 204 p.

131. NEILS, ELAINE M. *Reservation to City: Indian Migration and Federal Relocation*. 1971. x + 198 p.

132. MOLINE, NORMAN T. *Mobility and the Small Town, 1900-1930*. 1971. ix + 169 p.

133. SCHWIND, PAUL J. *Migration and Regional Development in the United States, 1950-1960*. 1971. x + 170 p.

134. PYLE, GERALD F. *Heart Disease, Cancer and Stroke in Chicago: A Geographical Analysis with Facilities, Plans for 1980*. 1971. ix + 292 p.

135. JOHNSON, JAMES F. *Renovated Waste Water: An Alternative Source of Municipal Water Supply in the United States*. 1971. ix + 155 p.

136. BUTZER, KARL W. *Recent History of an Ethiopian Delta: The Omo River and the Level of Lake Rudolf*. 1971. xvi + 184 p.

139. McMANIS, DOUGLAS R. *European Impressions of the New England Coast, 1497-1620*. 1972. viii + 147 p.

140. COHEN, YEHOSHUA S. *Diffusion of an Innovation in an Urban System: The Spread of Planned Regional Shopping Centers in the United States, 1949-1968*. 1972. ix + 136 p.

141. MITCHELL, NORA. *The Indian Hill-Station: Kodaikanal*. 1972. xii + 199 p.

142. PLATT, RUTHERFORD H. *The Open Space Decision Process: Spatial Allocation of Costs and Benefits*. 1972. xi + 189 p.

143. GOLANT, STEPHEN M. *The Residential Location and Spatial Behavior of the Elderly: A Canadian Example*. 1972. xv + 226 p.

144. PANNELL, CLIFTON W. *T'ai-Chung, T'ai-wan: Structure and Function*. 1973.xii + 200 p.

145. LANKFORD, PHILIP M. *Regional Incomes in the United States, 1929-1967: Level, Distribution, Stability, and Growth*. 1972. x + 137 p.

146. FREEMAN, DONALD B. *International Trade, Migration, and Capital Flows: A Quantitative Analysis of Spatial Economic Interaction*. 1973. xiv + 201 p.

147. MYERS, SARAH K. *Language Shift among Migrants to Lima, Peru*. 1973. xiii + 203 p.

148. JOHNSON, DOUGLAS L. *Jabal al-Akhdar, Cyrenaica: An Historical Geography of Settlement and Livelihood*. 1973. xii + 240 p.

149. YEUNG, YUE-MAN. *National Development Policy and Urban Transformation in Singapore: A Study of Public Housing and the Marketing System.* 1973. x + 204 p.

150. HALL, FRED L. *Location Criteria for High Schools: Student Transportation and Racial Integration.* 1973. xii + 156 p.

151. ROSENBERG, TERRY J. *Residence, Employment, and Mobility of Puerto Ricans in New York City.* 1974. xi + 230 p.

152. MIKESELL, MARVIN W., ed. *Geographers Abroad: Essays on the Problems and Prospects of Research in Foreign Areas.* 1973. ix + 296 p.

153. OSBORN, JAMES. *Area, Development Policy, and the Middle City in Malaysia.* 1974. x+ 291 p.

154. WACHT, WALTER F. *The Domestic Air Transportation Network of the United States.* 1974. ix + 98 p.

155. BERRY, BRIAN J. L. et al. *Land Use, Urban Form and Environmental Quality.* 1974. xxiii + 440 p.

156. MITCHELL, JAMES K. *Community Response to Coastal Erosion: Individual and Collective Adjustments to Hazard on the Atlantic Shore.* 1974. xii + 209 p.

157. COOK, GILLIAN P. *Spatial Dynamics of Business Growth in the Witwatersrand.* 1975. x + 144 p.

160. MEYER, JUDITH W. *Diffusion of an American Montessori Education.* 1975. xi + 97 p.

161. SCHMID, JAMES A. *Urban Vegetation: A Review and Chicago Case Study.* 1975. xii + 266 p.

162. LAMB, RICHARD F. *Metropolitan Impacts on Rural America.* 1975. xii + 196 p.

163. FEDOR, THOMAS STANLEY. *Patterns of Urban Growth in the Russian Empire during the Nineteenth Century.* 1975. xxv + 245 p.

164. HARRIS, CHAUNCY D. *Guide to Geographical Bibliographies and Reference Works in Russian or on the Soviet Union.* 1975. xviii + 478 p.

165. JONES, DONALD W. *Migration and Urban Unemployment in Dualistic Economic Development.* 1975. x + 174 p.

166. BEDNARZ, ROBERT S. *The Effect of Air Pollution on Property Value in Chicago.* 1975. viii + 111 p.

167. HANNEMANN, MANFRED. *The Diffusion of the Reformation in Southwestern Germany, 1518-1534.* 1975. ix + 235 p.

168. SUBLETT, MICHAEL D. *Farmers on the Road: Interfarm Migration and the Farming of Noncontiguous Lands in Three Midwestern Townships. 1939-1969.* 1975. xiii + 214 p.

169. STETZER, DONALD FOSTER. *Special Districts in Cook County: Toward a Geography of Local Government.* 1975. xi + 177 p.

171. SPODEK, HOWARD. *Urban-Rural Integration in Regional Development: A Case Study of Saurashtra, India—1800-1960.* 1976. xi + 144 p.

172. COHEN, YEHOSHUA S., and BRIAN J. L. BERRY. *Spatial Components of Manufacturing Change.* 1975. vi + 262 p.

173. HAYES, CHARLES R. *The Dispersed City: The Case of Piedmont, North Carolina.* 1976. ix + 157 p.

174. CARGO, DOUGLAS B. *Solid Wastes: Factors Influencing Generation Rates.* 1977. viii + 100 p.

175. GILLARD, QUENTIN. *Incomes and Accessibility: Metropolitan Labor Force Participation, Commuting, and Income Differentials in the United States, 1960-1970.* 1977. ix + 106 p.

176. MORGAN, DAVID J. *Patterns of Population Distribution: A Residential Preference Model and Its Dynamic.* 1978. xiii + 200 p.

177. STOKES, HOUSTON H., DONALD W. JONES, AND HUGH M. NEUBURGER. *Unemployment and Adjustment in the Labor Market: A Comparison between the Regional and National Responses.* 1975. ix + 125 p.

180. CARR, CLAUDIA J. *Pastoralism in Crisis. The Dasanetch and Their Ethiopian Lands.* 1977. xx + 319 p.

181. GOODWIN, GARY C. *Cherokees in Transition: A Study of Changing Culture and Environment Prior to 1775.* 1977. ix + 207 p.

182. KNIGHT, DAVID B. *A Capital for Canada: Conflict and Compromise in the Nineteenth Century.* 1977. xvii + 341 p.

183. HAIGH, MARTIN J. *The Evolution of Slopes on Artificial Landforms, Blaenavon, U.K.* 1978. xiv + 293 p.

184. FINK, L. DEE. *Listening to the Learner: An Exploratory Study of Personal Meaning in College Geography Courses.* 1977. ix + 186 p.

185. HELGREN, DAVID M. *Rivers of Diamonds: An Alluvial History of the Lower Vaal Basin, South Africa.* 1979. xix + 389 p.

186. BUTZER, KARL W., ed. *Dimensions of Human Geography: Essays on Some Familiar and Neglected Themes.* 1978. vii + 190 p.

187. MITSUHASHI, SETSUKO. *Japanese Commodity Flows.* 1978. x + 172 p.

188. CARIS, SUSAN L. *Community Attitudes toward Pollution.* 1978. xii + 211 p.

189. REES, PHILIP M.*Residential Patterns in American Cities: 1960.*1979. xvi +405 p.

190. KANNE, EDWARD A. *Fresh Food for Nicosia.* 1979. x + 106 p.

192. KIRCHNER, JOHN A. *Sugar and Seasonal Labor Migration: The Case of Tucumán, Argentina.* 1980. xii + 174 p.

193. HARRIS, CHAUNCY D., AND JEROME D. FELLMANN. *International List of Geographical Serials, Third Edition, 1980.* 1980. vi + 457 p.

194. HARRIS, CHAUNCY D. *Annotated World List of Selected Current Geographical Serials, Fourth Edition. 1980.* 1980. iv + 165 p.

195. LEUNG, CHI-KEUNG. *China: Railway Patterns and National Goals.* 1980. xv + 243 p.

196. LEUNG, CHI-KEUNG, AND NORTON S. GINSBURG, eds. *China: Urbanizations and National Development.* 1980. ix + 283 p.

197. DAICHES, SOL. *People in Distress: A Geographical Perspective on Psychological Well-being.* 1981. xiv + 199 p.

198. JOHNSON, JOSEPH T. *Location and Trade Theory: Industrial Location, Comparative Advantage, and the Geographic Pattern of Production in the United States.* 1981. xi + 107 p.

199-200. STEVENSON, ARTHUR J. *The New York-Newark Air Freight System.* 1982. xvi + 440 p.

201. LICATE, JACK A. *Creation of a Mexican Landscape: Territorial Organization and Settlement in the Eastern Puebla Basin, 1520-1605.* 1981. x + 143 p.

202. RUDZITIS, GUNDARS. *Residential Location Determinants of the Older Population.* 1982. x + 117 p.

203. LIANG, ERNEST P. *China: Railways and Agricultural Development, 1875-1935.* 1982. xi + 186 p.

204. DAHMANN, DONALD C. *Locals and Cosmopolitans: Patterns of Spatial Mobility during the Transition from Youth to Early Adulthood.* 1982. xiii + 146 p.

205. FOOTE, KENNETH E. *Color in Public Spaces: Toward a Communication-Bases Theory of the Urban Built Environment.* 1983. xiv + 153 p.

206. HARRIS, CHAUNCY D. *Bibliography of Geography. Part II: Regional. Volume 1. The United States of America.* 1984. viii + 178 p.

207-208. WHEATLEY, PAUL. *Nagara and Commandery: Origins of the Southeast Asian Urban Traditions.* 1983. xv + 472 p.

209. SAARINEN, THOMAS F., DAVID SEAMON, AND JAMES L. SELL, eds. *Environmental Perception and Behavior: An Inventory and Prospect.* 1984. x + 263 p.

210. WESCOAT, JAMES L., JR. *Integrated Water Development: Water Use and Conservation Practice in Western Colorado.* 1984. xi + 239 p.

211. DEMKO, GEORGE J., AND ROLAND J. FUCHS, eds. *Geographical Studies on the Soviet Union: Essays in Honor of Chauncy D. Harris.* 1984. vii + 294 p.

212. HOLMES, ROLAND C. *Irrigation in Southern Peru: The Chili Basin.* 1986. ix + 199 p.

213. EDMONDS, RICHARD LOUIS. *Northern Frontiers of Qing China and Tokugawa Japan: A Comparative Study of Frontier Policy.* 1985. xi + 209 p.

214. FREEMAN, DONALD B., AND GLEN B. NORCLIFFE. *Rural Enterprise in Kenya: Development and Spatial Organization of the Nonfarm Sector.* 1985. xiv + 180 p.

215. COHEN, YEHOSHUA S., AND AMNON SHINAR. *Neighborhoods and Friendship Networks:A Study of Three Residential Neighborhoods in Jerusalem.*1985. ix +137 p.

216. OBERMEYER, NANCY J. *Bureaucrats, Clients, and Geography: The Bailly Nuclear Power Plant Battle in Northern Indiana.* 1989. x + 135 p.

217-218. CONZEN, MICHAEL P., ed. *World Patterns of Modern Urban Change: Essays in Honor of Chauncy D. Harris.* 1986. x + 479 p.

219. KOMOGUCHI, YOSHIMI. *Agricultural Systems in the Tamil Nadu: A Case Study of Peruvalanallur Village.* 1986. xvi + 175 p.

220. GINSBURG, NORTON, JAMES OSBORN, AND GRANT BLANK. *Geographic Perspectives on the Wealth of Nations.* 1986. ix + 1331 p.

221. BAYLSON, JOSHUA C. *Territorial Allocation by Imperial Rivalry: The Human Legacy in the Near East.* 1987. xi + 138 p.

222. DORN, MARILYN APRIL. *The Administrative Partitioning of Costa Rica.* 1989. xi + 126 p.

224. PLATT, RUTHERFORD H., SHEILA G. PELCZARSKI, AND BARBARA K. BURBANK, eds. *Cities on the Beach: Management Issues of Developed Coastal Barriers.* 1987. vii + 324 p.

225. LATZ, GIL. *Agricultural Development in Japan: The Land Improvement District in Concept and Practice.* 1989. viii + 135 p.

226. GRITZNER, JEFFREY A. *The West African Sahel: Human Agency and Environmental Change.* 1988. xii + 170 p.

227. MURPHY, ALEXANDER B. *The Regional Dynamics of Language Differentiation in Belgium: A Study in Cultural-Political Geography.* 1988. xiii + 249 p.